W9-BSQ-611

HORSE GAITS,
BALANCE
AND MOVEMENT

HORSE GAITS,
BALANCE
AND MOVEMENT

Susan E. Harris

Howell Book House
Published by Wiley Publishing, Inc., New York, NY

Library of Congress Cataloging-in-Publication Data:
Harris, Susan E.
Horse gaits, balance and movement/ Susan E. Harris.
p.cm
Includes index.
ISBN 0-87605-955-8
1. Horses—paces, gaits, etc.   I. Title.
SF289.H37   1993
636.1'089276—dc20   92-16332
CIP
Manufactured in the United States of America.

18 17 16 15 14 13 12 11

This book is dedicated, with love, respect and gratitude,

to all my teachers

and to the horses who continue to teach us all.

CONTENTS

FOREWORD

Privileged enough to have been one of the first to read the manuscript of *Horse Gaits, Balance and Movement,* I must sincerely congratulate my dear friend Susan Harris for her wonderful new book.

At last, a competent author has spent the necessary time to elaborate clearly on what is known to be the essence of true horsemanship. Equestrians have always had a common denominator in the love of horses, but how many have truly studied and thoroughly considered the hippomechanism of this so noble animal?

For all of us, Susan Harris has, in the following pages, condensed, in a very pleasant format with superb illustrations, the essential knowledge that each horseman and each horsewoman must acquire. It is most important to comprehend well the horse's body and its various functions to better pursue his education in a very natural and logical manner. The study of conformation reveals what would be the most suitable discipline for the horse to follow; the knowledge of the bone structure will indicate where the power and weakness reside; the understanding of the interaction of all the congeneric and antagonistic muscles will indicate how to overcome a possible deficiency in the horse's locomotion, or way of going; and the proper shoeing will provide exactitude and comfort at the various gaits. In the last chapter Susan Harris explains, through proper usage of the natural aids, how the rider should adapt his or her body to avoid involuntarily affecting the horse's movement.

Horse Gaits, Balance and Movement will always have a place of choice in my library, and I will refer to it often to learn and relearn all the valuable lessons of Susan Harris.

François Lemaire de Ruffieu
Gloucester, Virginia

PREFACE

There are thousands of books on the horse and his riding and training, going all the way back to Xenophon, many of them timeless classics. The best books have always been based on the author's practical experience with horses and grounded in classical theory, and this book starts from the same premise.

This book arose out of my experiences in learning, training, showing and judging, but especially from my teaching. I travel to conduct clinics in all parts of the United States, and I get all kinds of horses and riders, all seats and styles of riding, in my clinics. While the various types of horses and disciplines sometimes seem sharply divided, I have found that good movement and good use of the body (for both horse and rider) are a common basis for all forms of horsemanship. The best horsemen, trainers and teachers in all disciplines understand the horse's structure and mechanism, his natural balance and way of moving, and how he should best use

himself to do the particular job required in that specialty. While a western pleasure horse, a gaited American Saddlebred, a dressage horse and a Grand Prix jumper may seem poles apart, they are still horses, with the same anatomy, locomotion and basic horse nature.

Today there are more opportunities for using and enjoying our horses, for competition, and for learning about horses than ever before. Unfortunately, our understanding and knowledge has not always kept pace with our enthusiasm for new activities and for competition. Many riders today put in hours of practice and have had extensive competitive coaching, but have never been taught the basics of horse movement or the reasons behind the practice. Understanding basic theory makes good riding and training simpler, clearer and less frustrating. So many of the horse and rider problems I see, and the questions I am asked, are based on the horse's structure, movement and nature, and the problems that arise when we try to get him to carry us and do things our way without knowing enough about the horse and his ways. It is easy enough to recognize a movement problem when a rider cannot sit to his horse's trot or the horse will not take a left lead, but many behavior problems and attitude problems originate there, too. A horse that tosses his head, bucks, runs away or pokes along like a slug is not deliberately "being a jerk" or plotting against his rider—often he is simply finding it very hard to move comfortably under his rider, and being animal, he can only tell us by his behavior. Such horses often become much happier, more cooperative and easier to ride when they are helped to move better and as the rider learns to make it easier for his horse to move well. They also may become sounder, stronger and more beautiful to ride or to watch. I hope this book will make some of the basic knowledge and "whys" more readily available to all riders.

In our highly competitive horse world today, we are too often prone to believe that "more is better." This has led to excesses and unsound and harmful practices that are not based on good movement and body-use principles. For instance, while a western pleasure horse is supposed to have a low, relaxed head carriage, getting your horse to carry his head lower than anyone else does not make him a better pleasure ride, and making him drag his nose on the ground will not produce the "ultimate" pleasure horse; instead, it will ruin his movement and eventually damage the horse. The problem gets even more serious when an extreme and unfunctional form of movement becomes popular and is rewarded by judges and sought after by trainers, riders and eventually breeders—all in a quest for high score awards. This leads to abusive training methods and can affect the whole future of a breed or discipline. Some recent examples are the soring of Walking Horses to produce the exaggerated "big lick" running walk; the unnaturally low head carriage and slow movement demanded in western pleasure classes in recent years; the overbent carriage and "running" gaits that have been all too common in certain breed pleasure classes; and the hollow back and strained, artificial, high action seen in some park horses. Every breed and discipline (including dressage!) has had its own fads and follies, so no one can afford to be complacent. I hope this book will help riders, trainers, judges and breeders to base their riding, training and selection on the principles of good movement, and will provide some guidelines when looking at trends, techniques and innovations and how far they should go.

In understanding horse movement and the best way to help the horse develop his movement, I believe that classical dressage methods can be helpful in any discipline and are the best in the long run. After all, dressage is essentially concerned with developing the horse's body, strength, suppleness and ability to move well, and it has been studied for centuries for just this purpose. However, as dressage (and especially competitive dressage) has become a more popular specialty in this country, I have to be clear about what I mean when I say "dressage" can help any horse. Good, functional training, based on classical principles, starts with understanding and improving the horse's use of his body; this kind of dressage is truly classical and, intelligently applied, will benefit any horse in any discipline. However, there are aspects of dressage competition and certain exercises that are not very useful to other disciplines and can even be dangerous when taken out of context. Trying to apply "dressage work" superficially and without understanding (for example, overdoing lateral movements and "suppling" exercises; excessive use of a driving seat, sitting trot and strong contact; or trying to teach your hunter to piaffe!) can lead to confusion and frustration and may even spoil some horses' movement. It is risky to take dressage movements, like the shoulder-in, out of context and try to apply them to a horse that has not had the progressive preparation that is integral to good, classical dressage work. If it makes your horse move worse, it's bad dressage anyway. If you ride in another discipline but feel that some classical dressage methods might help your horse, you may need to seek out an instructor or trainer who is familiar with your field as well as with classical dressage, and be sure that he knows that you are primarily interested in improving your horse's movement within his specialty. I feel that it is good for any rider, in any specialty, to have some good dressage experience. It is important that to get the right experience—solid basics that apply to all your riding and training—and

not fall into the trap of mistaking the superficial trappings for the basic essentials.

I hope this book will be useful to those who ride, teach, train, show, judge and select horses, and especially to the average rider who wants to enjoy and appreciate his horse and the way they move together.

Nobody learns without help and inspiration, and I would like to acknowledge the great teachers who have helped me along the road; both those I have known and worked with personally and those I have known only through their writings. I would especially like to say "Thank you" to the following:

To my earliest instructors, Captain Samuel A. Hendrickson, Leah Underwood and Nancy Whicher, who all taught the "whys" as well as the "hows" and based their teaching on sound and simple theory.

To George Morris, who gave me an organized and logical basis for learning and teaching, and who proves that it is possible to reach the top while remaining a true horseman.

To Carol Loomis, who gave me a deeper appreciation of the horse's mechanism, and how simple good riding really is when we work correctly.

To Sally Swift, who taught me about awareness, freedom and using the body well, whether in horse or human, and whose Centered Riding principles continue to enrich my life and lead to greater discoveries.

To François LeMaire de Ruffieu, who was kind enough to review the manuscript and art for this book from the standpoint of classical horsemanship, and who clarified many points for me. Where this book is correct, he has helped it to be so, and any errors are the author's own, not his.

And especially, to all the horses I have loved and learned from.

SUSAN E. HARRIS

1

WHY LEARN ABOUT GAITS, BALANCE AND MOVEMENT?

Horses *move!* It's what they do best, and it is why we ride, drive, train or just watch horses instead of eating them. Movement is what caused the horse to develop from the fox-sized eohippus of 55 million years ago into the modern horse and what allowed the horse to escape from predators armed with tooth and claw. The horse's movement has always attracted man. It has made him useful to man as a beast of burden, for travel, work, war and sport, and has shaped the history of many peoples. Over the centuries the horse and his movement have been an inspiration

FIGURE 1 *From Eohippus to modern horse.*

FIGURE 2 *All horses move naturally; not all move equally well.*

to artists, poets and writers. "And God took a handful of West Wind and created the horse . . ." says the Koran. Today, when most people ride for sport or pleasure, the horse's ability to move is his most essential trait. It is what makes him useful, able and beautiful.

All horses have their natural basic movements. A foal can walk, trot and gallop within hours of its birth. The horse knows how to be a horse without human help. However, when we ride, drive, train and judge horses, we soon discover that not all horses move equally well. Some are talented, others handicapped. Some are more suited for a particular kind of job or way of moving than others. Some are easy to ride and train, others difficult.

When we ride horses, we are asking them to adapt to a task nature never intended them to do. They do it remarkably well, but carrying a rider changes their balance, their way of going and their natural movements. (Just try carrying a load of 15 to 20 percent of your weight on your shoulders—especially if it is live weight, with a mind of its own!) Besides the weight of the rider (who may or may not stay balanced), the horse is controlled and directed by the rider. He is asked to move at a particular gait and speed, in a certain direction, and even to carry himself in a certain fashion. He may not start, stop or turn however and whenever he pleases. Much of the time, he cannot understand why we want him to collect himself, move forward or sideways or jump this obstacle or perform that maneuver. Some riders are better than others at communicating with their horses, but no

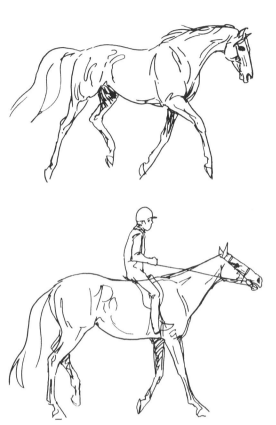

FIGURE 3 *Horses move easily on their own, but may have difficulty moving under a rider.*

rider speaks perfect "horse language." It is a tribute to the kindness and generosity of horses that they carry us as well as they do, and that they keep on trying.

When we ride and train horses, we have a responsibility to work with their nature, their mechanism and their natural movement. Good movement is natural, easy, comfortable and efficient for horse and rider; it is also

FIGURE 4 *Horse and rider moving well, in harmony, vs. ugly and damaging movement.*

beautiful. Bad movement is ugly, hard to ride and uncomfortable and damaging to the horse. When we ask horses for maximum performance in any discipline, they will only be able to achieve their full potential through good movement. This takes some knowledge on the part of the rider, along with good riding. It is hard to ride well and impossible to train well if you don't understand how the horse moves and what makes good and bad movement. The rider must learn about movement in order to help his horse carry him in the best possible way.

If you show, judge, breed or select horses to buy, movement is of great importance. Success in the show ring creates popularity and can have a great influence on the way horses are ridden, trained and bred to move. Some breeds of dogs have been damaged because breeders selected their stock for one extreme characteristic while ignoring functional movement; the result has been an in-herited tendency toward hip dysplasia, arthritis and early breakdowns. Some similar trends have hurt certain breeds of horses, although the demands of performance usually steer horse breeders back in the direction of functional conformation. Few people care to keep a lame horse just because he is pretty to look at.

There are over two hundred breeds and types of horses, and many different disciplines and styles of riding. However, the horse's basic mechanism and nature are still the same, whether he is a racing Thoroughbred, a Clydesdale, a working cow horse or a miniature horse. By learning how the horse's body works and how he moves naturally, we can avoid misguided and damaging efforts as we work to help him carry us with the best movement he is capable of. Let's remember that a horse without a rider is still a horse, but a rider without a horse is only a human.

2

BASIC STRUCTURE AND ANATOMY

In order to understand how horses move, we need to know what the horse's structure is like under the skin. The bones are the framework and the levers; the muscles and tendons move the bones. The "points" or parts of the horse are the names of the surface landmarks of the horse's body. Knowing basic anatomy helps us relate the major structures to what they do and what we see on the surface. However, it isn't necessary to learn all the technical names of the bones and muscles in order to have a basic understanding of horse gaits and movement. If you find the anatomical details a bit overwhelming, you may prefer to skim through this chapter or use the diagrams for reference. Of course, the more you learn about the horse's structure and physiology, the better you can understand what happens during movement and in the stresses and strains that can lead to unsoundness.

THE SKELETAL STRUCTURE

The horse's skeleton contains approximately 205 bones. It includes the axial skeleton, which includes the skull, spinal column, ribs and breastbone, and the appendicular skeleton, made up of the pelvis and limbs. The long bones (leg bones) are levers that support and move the body. The short bones (like those found in the joints) absorb concussion. Flat bones such as the ribs, pelvis and skull bones protect vital organs and provide a large area for the attachment of muscles. Irregular bones of the spinal column protect the spinal cord. Bones are held together by ligaments, while muscles are attached to bones by tendons.

Joints are where bones meet bones. Most joints permit varying degrees of movement; others, like the joints of the skull, allow no movement. Ligaments bind the bones together with strong connective tissue. The lig-

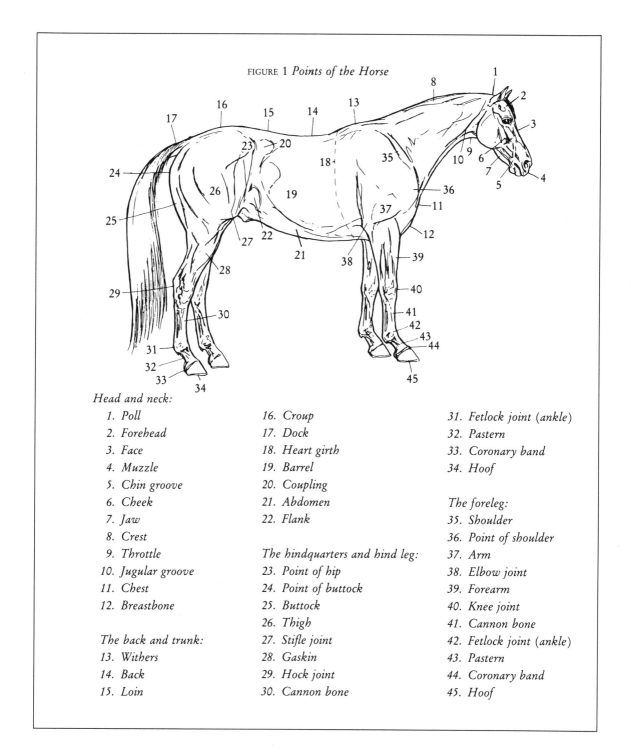

FIGURE 1 *Points of the Horse*

Head and neck:

1. Poll
2. Forehead
3. Face
4. Muzzle
5. Chin groove
6. Cheek
7. Jaw
8. Crest
9. Throttle
10. Jugular groove
11. Chest
12. Breastbone

The back and trunk:

13. Withers
14. Back
15. Loin

16. Croup
17. Dock
18. Heart girth
19. Barrel
20. Coupling
21. Abdomen
22. Flank

The hindquarters and hind leg:

23. Point of hip
24. Point of buttock
25. Buttock
26. Thigh
27. Stifle joint
28. Gaskin
29. Hock joint
30. Cannon bone

31. Fetlock joint (ankle)
32. Pastern
33. Coronary band
34. Hoof

The foreleg:

35. Shoulder
36. Point of shoulder
37. Arm
38. Elbow joint
39. Forearm
40. Knee joint
41. Cannon bone
42. Fetlock joint (ankle)
43. Pastern
44. Coronary band
45. Hoof

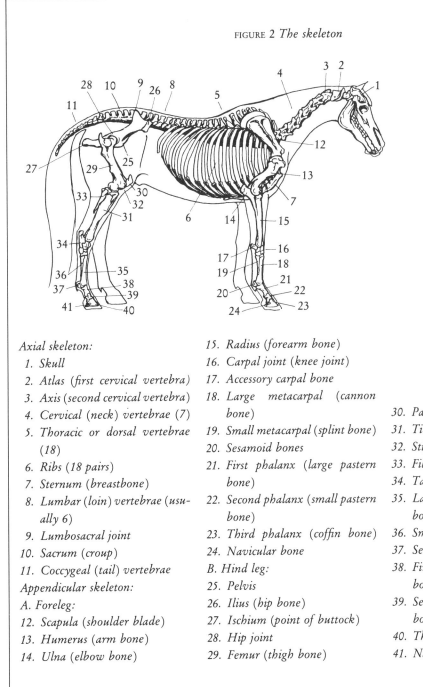

FIGURE 2 *The skeleton*

Axial skeleton:

1. *Skull*
2. *Atlas (first cervical vertebra)*
3. *Axis (second cervical vertebra)*
4. *Cervical (neck) vertebrae (7)*
5. *Thoracic or dorsal vertebrae (18)*
6. *Ribs (18 pairs)*
7. *Sternum (breastbone)*
8. *Lumbar (loin) vertebrae (usually 6)*
9. *Lumbosacral joint*
10. *Sacrum (croup)*
11. *Coccygeal (tail) vertebrae*

Appendicular skeleton:

A. Foreleg:

12. *Scapula (shoulder blade)*
13. *Humerus (arm bone)*
14. *Ulna (elbow bone)*
15. *Radius (forearm bone)*
16. *Carpal joint (knee joint)*
17. *Accessory carpal bone*
18. *Large metacarpal (cannon bone)*
19. *Small metacarpal (splint bone)*
20. *Sesamoid bones*
21. *First phalanx (large pastern bone)*
22. *Second phalanx (small pastern bone)*
23. *Third phalanx (coffin bone)*
24. *Navicular bone*

B. Hind leg:

25. *Pelvis*
26. *Ilius (hip bone)*
27. *Ischium (point of buttock)*
28. *Hip joint*
29. *Femur (thigh bone)*
30. *Patella (kneecap)*
31. *Tibia*
32. *Stifle joint*
33. *Fibula*
34. *Tarsal joint (hock joint)*
35. *Large metatarsal (cannon bone)*
36. *Small metatarsal (splint bone)*
37. *Sesamoid bones*
38. *First phalanx (large pastern bone)*
39. *Second phalanx (small pastern bone)*
40. *Third phalanx (coffin bone)*
41. *Navicular bone*

BASIC STRUCTURE AND ANATOMY

aments of a joint form a joint capsule, which is lubricated with synovial fluid. The articulating surfaces of bones (joint surfaces) are covered with cartilage, which is smooth, slippery and softer than bone and lessens concussion and friction.

Joints absorb shock as well as allowing movement. The flexion, or bending, of a joint helps to absorb shock, as does the cushioning effect of the cartilage and synovial fluid. The many small bones of the knee and hock joints help to dissipate concussion. The forelegs are not attached to the axial skeleton by a bony joint (as are human arms); instead they are connected only by a "sling" of muscles. This "shoulder sling" also acts as an important shock absorber.

Each joint has an important role in movement. The major joints and their functions are described below:

Axial Skeleton

- The mandibular (jaw) joint permits opening and closing of the mouth.
- The atlas (poll) joint allows flexion and extension of the head at the atlas (first cervical vertebra); a key joint in the horse's balance and response to the bridle.
- The axis joint (between the first and second cervical vertebrae) permits the head to flex laterally (side to side); this is where true lateral flexion of the poll takes place.
- The joints of the remaining cervical vertebrae allow up and down and side-to-side flexion and extension of the neck.
- The joints of the dorsal (back) and lumbar

(loin) vertebrae have fairly limited ability to flex and extend up and down and laterally because of the shape of the vertebrae and the way they articulate. The horse's back is more rigid than that of many other animals.

- The lumbosacral joint is found between the last lumbar vertebra and the sacrum (croup), which is attached to the ilium, or wings, of the pelvis. A key joint, as it allows the horse to flex the loin and bring his hind legs forward for movement and balance.
- The coccygeal joints (joints of the tail) allow very free movement up, down and sideways; they reflect the position and tension or relaxation of the back.
- The ribs can flex up and down with a slight rotation during breathing. The flexibility of the long, thin rib bones and the costal cartilage make this possible.

Appendicular Skeleton
Joints of the Foreleg

- Shoulder sling. The shoulders are not joined to the trunk by a bony joint but by a "sling" of muscles. They glide freely over the ribs and rotate forward and backward. The shoulders can tilt sideways to reach outward with the whole foreleg or to bring the foreleg inward for lateral movements.
- The shoulder joint is between the shoulder blade and humerus (arm bone). Flexion and extension are mostly forward and backward, moving the whole foreleg, with limited lateral movement.

FIGURE 3 *The joints*

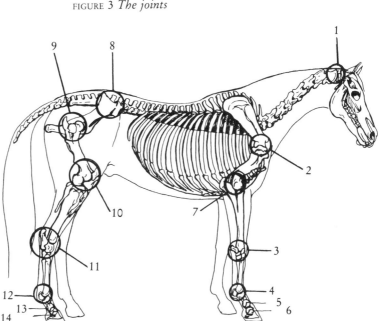

1. *Poll (atlas) joint*
2. *Shoulder joint*
3. *Carpal (knee) joint*
4. *Fetlock (ankle) joint*
5. *Pastern joint*
6. *Coffin joint*
7. *Elbow joint*
8. *Lumbosacral joint*
9. *Hip joint*
10. *Stifle joint*
11. *Tarsal (hock) joint*
12. *Fetlock (ankle) joint*
13. *Pastern joint*
14. *Coffin joint*

- The elbow joint—between the humerus (arm bone) and ulna and radius (elbow and forearm bones)—flexes and extends forward and backward only.
- The knee (carpal) joint—made up of seven bones between the radius (forearm) and metacarpal bones (cannon and splint bones), flexes forward and backward only.
- The fetlock joint (ankle) is located between the metacarpal (cannon) bone, sesamoid bones and first phalanx (long pastern bone). Flexes only forward and backward; absorbs shock by allowing the pastern to sink under the weight of the horse.
- The pastern joint—between the first and second phalanx (long and short pastern

bones)—has very little movement, mostly forward and backward.
- The coffin joint, between the second and third phalanx (short pastern and coffin bones), has very little movement, mostly forward and backward.
- The navicular joint, found between the navicular bone, coffin bone and short pastern bone, allows little movement but cushions the deep digital flexor tendon, which passes over the navicular bone and attaches to the underside of the coffin bone; it absorbs shock at each stride.

Joints of the Hind Leg

- The hip joint is located between the pelvis

and femur (thigh bone); it is a ball and socket joint. Most movement is forward and backward, but some lateral (side to side) movement is also possible. It moves the whole hind leg.

- The stifle joint is found between the femur (thigh bone) and patella (kneecap) and tibia; movement is forward and backward.
- The hock (tarsal) joint is made up of six bones between the tibia and the metatarsals (cannon and splint bones). It flexes only forward and backward. The hock and stifle are reciprocal joints; that is, when one flexes or extends, the other must do the same.
- Fetlock joint—same as in foreleg.
- Pastern joint—same as in foreleg.
- Coffin joint—same as in foreleg.
- Navicular joint—same as in foreleg.

LIGAMENTS AND MUSCLES

Ligaments, which bind bones together, are made of strong, slightly elastic connective tissue. Besides holding the bones together, some ligaments have special functions. The powerful cervical ligament (also called the nuchal ligament), which runs from the poll and the bones of the neck to the spines of the withers, allows the horse to use his head and neck to change the balance of his whole body. The dorsal ligament system, which runs along the top line from the poll to the tail, includes the cervical ligament and those of the spine, croup and upper pelvis. These play an important part in the way the horse uses its back in movement and changes of balance, and in carrying a rider. Collateral ligaments are the system of ligaments that bind the bones of a joint together, such as the collateral ligaments of the knee. ("Lateral" refers to ligaments on the outside of a leg; "medial" to those on the inside.) Capsular ligaments are those that form an enclosed joint capsule. The suspensory ligaments of the lower leg are important in stabilizing the leg bones and in absorbing shock during movement.

Muscles move bones and aid in other vital functions such as breathing and heartbeat; skeletal muscles are those that move the bones. Muscles are attached to bones by tendons, which are like cables of tough, dense connective tissue. Fascia is a thin, tough sheet of connective tissue.

Muscles work by contraction, or shortening of the muscle fibers, followed by relaxation, which allows the muscle fibers to return to their normal length. The contraction of muscles, acting on tendon cables, bone levers and joint hinges, makes motion possible. Muscles can only pull on bones; they cannot push, so they work in pairs. One group of muscles bends or flexes a joint (flexor muscles), and an opposing group extends or straightens it (extensor muscles).

Because the muscles lie over each other in layers, one diagram cannot show all the skeletal muscles. The following diagrams show some of the most important muscles for movement.

The tendons and ligaments that run down the front and back of the horse's legs form

FIGURE 4 *Major ligaments*

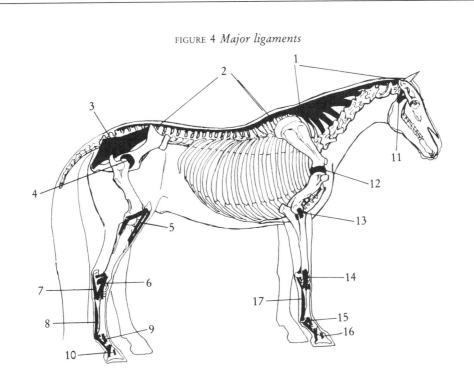

1. *Cervical (nuchal) ligament (dorsal ligament system)*
2. *Supraspinous ligament (dorsal ligament system)*
3. *Lateral sacroiliac and sacrosciatic ligaments (dorsal ligament system)*
4. *Capsular ligament of hip joint*
5. *Lateral and medial patellar ligaments*
6. *Lateral collateral ligament of tarsal joint*
7. *Plantar ligament*
8. *Hind suspensory ligament*
9. *Lateral collateral ligament of fetlock joint*
10. *Suspensory ligament of navicular bone*
11. *Lateral ligaments of jaw joint*
12. *Capsular ligament of shoulder joint*
13. *Lateral collateral ligaments of elbow joint*
14. *Lateral collateral ligament of carpal joint*
15. *Lateral collateral sesamoidan ligament*
16. *Lateral collateral ligament of coffin joint*
17. *Suspensory ligament*

the stay apparatus, which keeps the bones aligned even when the muscles are relaxed and allows the horse to rest while standing up. These structures, along with the leg mus-cles, absorb shock and contribute to a spring effect as each foot leaves the ground.

The tendons and ligaments of the lower leg are important in flexing and extending the

FIGURE 5 *Skeletal muscles*   FIGURE 6 *Superficial (outer) muscles (opposite)*

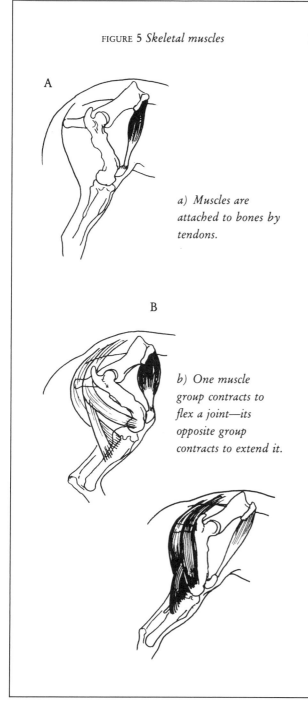

A

B

a) *Muscles are attached to bones by tendons.*

b) *One muscle group contracts to flex a joint—its opposite group contracts to extend it.*

1. *Masseter (jaw muscle—chewing)*
2. *Sternocephalic (sternum to head—lowers head)*
3. *Brachiocephalic (arm to head—extends forearm, lowers head)*
4. *Rhomboid (lifts head)*
5. *Splenius (lifts head)*
6. *Cervical (neck) part of serratus ventralis (levator angulae scapulae) (shoulder sling, lifts rib cage, turns neck)*
7. *Thoracic (rib) part of serratus ventralis (levator angulae scapulae) (shoulder sling, rotates shoulder blade)*
8. *Trapezius (tilts shoulder blade in lateral movement; rotates shoulder)*
9. *Deltoid (rotates shoulder blade)*
10. *Latissimus dorsi (long side muscle of back)*
11. *Triceps (long head and lateral head—extend elbow and rotate shoulder)*
12. *Posterior deep pectoral (back end of deep chest muscle)*
13. *Extensor carpi radialis (extends knee)*
14. *Common digital extensor (extends lower leg)*
15. *Ulnaris lateralis (flexes foreleg)*
16. *Deep digital flexor (flexes lower leg)*
17. *External abdominal oblique (aids in breathing, flexes ribs laterally)*
18. *External intercostal (aids in breathing)*
19. *Lumbardorsal fascia (strong, thin connective tissue)*
20. *Gluteal fascia (connective tissue)*
21. *Superficial gluteal (moves thigh)*

FIGURE 6 *Superficial (outer) muscles*

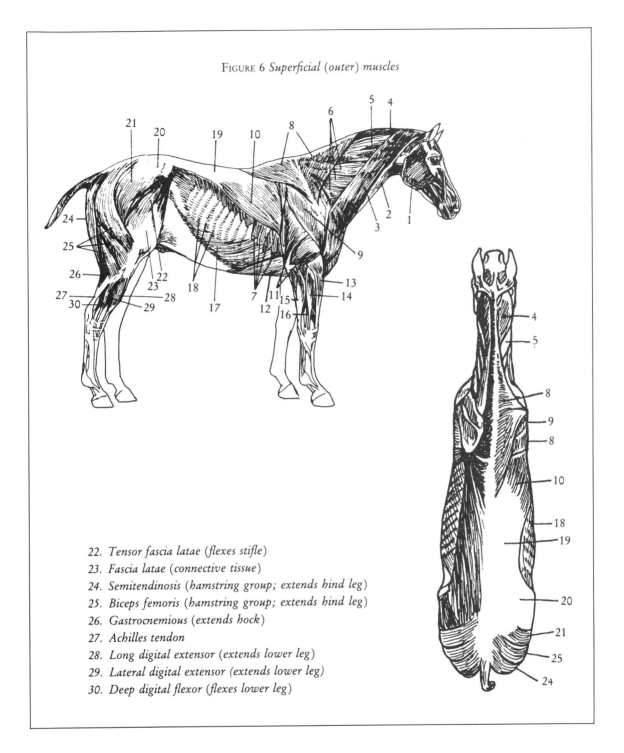

22. *Tensor fascia latae (flexes stifle)*
23. *Fascia latae (connective tissue)*
24. *Semitendinosis (hamstring group; extends hind leg)*
25. *Biceps femoris (hamstring group; extends hind leg)*
26. *Gastrocnemious (extends hock)*
27. *Achilles tendon*
28. *Long digital extensor (extends lower leg)*
29. *Lateral digital extensor (extends lower leg)*
30. *Deep digital flexor (flexes lower leg)*

BASIC STRUCTURE AND ANATOMY

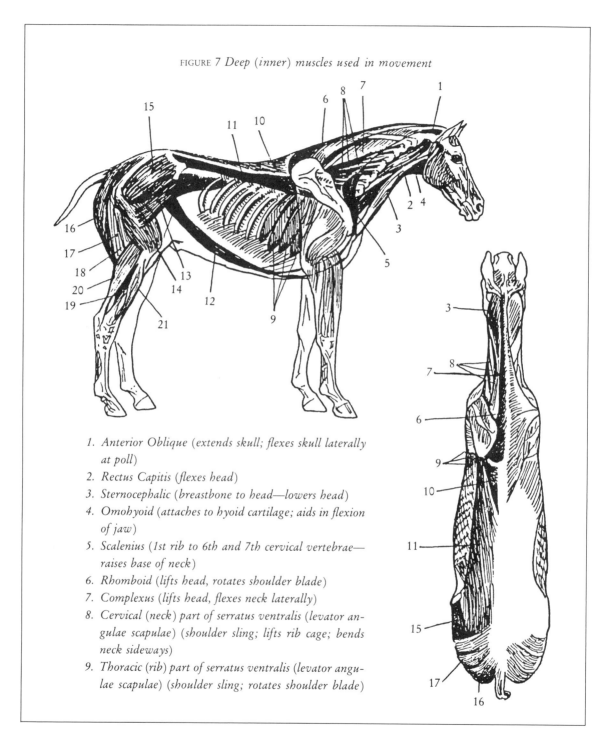

FIGURE 7 *Deep (inner) muscles used in movement*

1. *Anterior Oblique (extends skull; flexes skull laterally at poll)*
2. *Rectus Capitis (flexes head)*
3. *Sternocephalic (breastbone to head—lowers head)*
4. *Omohyoid (attaches to hyoid cartilage; aids in flexion of jaw)*
5. *Scalenius (1st rib to 6th and 7th cervical vertebrae— raises base of neck)*
6. *Rhomboid (lifts head, rotates shoulder blade)*
7. *Complexus (lifts head, flexes neck laterally)*
8. *Cervical (neck) part of serratus ventralis (levator angulae scapulae) (shoulder sling; lifts rib cage; bends neck sideways)*
9. *Thoracic (rib) part of serratus ventralis (levator angulae scapulae) (shoulder sling; rotates shoulder blade)*

FIGURE 7 *Deep (inner) muscles used in movement* (continued)

10. *Spinalis dorsi (connects spines of dorsal vertebrae)*
11. *Longissimus dorsi (long muscle of back; pelvis to cervical vertebrae)*
12. *Rectus abdominus (pelvis to breastbone; flexes lumbosacral joint; rounds back)*
13. *Iliopsoas (under side of lumbar spine to femur; flexes lumbosacral joint; draws femur and hind leg forward)*
14. *Vastus lateralis (quadriceps group—flexes hind leg; draws hind leg forward)*
15. *Medial gluteal (extends hind leg)*
16. *Semitendinosis (hamstring group; extends hind leg)*
17. *Semimembranosis (hamstring group; extends hind leg)*
18. *Biceps femoris (hamstring group; extends hind leg)*
19. *Deep digital flexor (extends hock joint)*
20. *Gastrocnemius (extends hock joint)*
21. *Long digital extensor (flexes hock joint; extends foot)*

leg, in absorbing shock, and in the check-and-stay apparatus of the front and hind leg. They also provide a spring effect as the foot leaves the ground. The tendons and ligaments of the lower foreleg and hind leg are essentially the same, although the knee (carpal) and hock (tarsal) joints are quite different.

The special structure of the horse's hoof supports the weight of his body, absorbs shock, provides traction and helps to pump the blood back up the leg to the heart. The outer wall of the hoof is made up of insensi-tive laminae, or hairlike tubules of protein, which intermesh with the sensitive laminae that grow from the surface of the coffin bone. The bones of the foot are suspended inside the hard but flexible structure of the outer wall. The corium lies beneath the coronary band; the hoof wall grows downward from it, like a fingernail from the nail bed.

The sole of the foot is concave and the outer layer is insensitive; a layer of sensitive sole lies closer to the inner bone structure. At the ground surface, the white line marks the dividing line between the wall and the sole. The wall bends backward at an angle at each end, forming the V-shaped bars, which aid in support and expansion of the foot. The frog is a rubbery structure at the ground surface that absorbs shock and helps prevent slipping. Inside the foot and above the frog lies the digital cushion, which contains major blood vessels of the foot. With each step, the horse compresses the frog and digital cushion and pumps the blood back up the leg toward the heart. The cleft is the crack down the center of the frog; the commissures are the spaces between the frog and the sole. The bulbs of the heels are formed by the flexible lateral cartilage that grows from the upper edges of the coffin bone.

Deep inside the foot, the deep digital flexor tendon passes underneath the navicular bone and attaches to the under surface of the coffin bone. Both the tendon and the navicular joint are cushioned by the navicular bursa, a small fluid-filled sac. The common digital extensor tendon attaches to the upper front of the coffin bone.

FIGURE 8 *Stay apparatus of the front and hind legs*

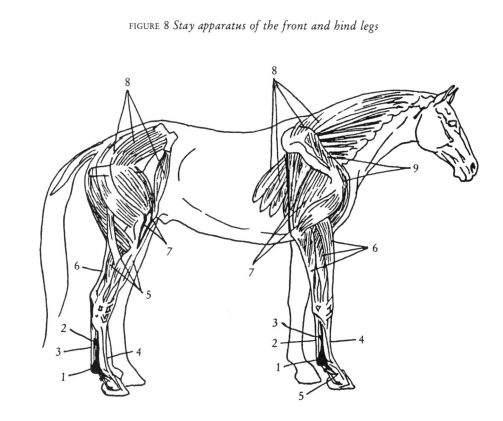

A. *Foreleg stay apparatus*
1. *Suspensory ligament*
2. *Flexor tendons (deep digital and superficial)*
3. *Carpal check ligament*
4. *Common digital extensor tendon*
5. *Deep digital flexor tendon*
6. *Forearm muscles*
7. *Triceps muscles*
8. *Muscles of shoulder sling*
9. *Shoulder muscles*

B. *Hind leg stay apparatus*
1. *Suspensory ligament*
2. *Flexor tendons (deep digital and superficial)*
3. *Tarsal check ligament*
4. *Common digital extensor tendon*
5. *Gaskin muscles*
6. *Achilles tendon*
7. *Patellar (stifle) ligaments*
8. *Muscles of hindquarters*

FIGURE 9 *Structures of the lower leg and foot*

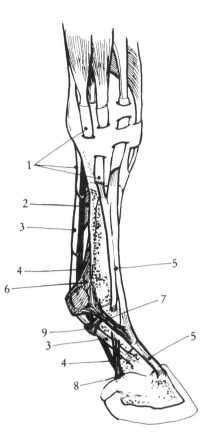

A. *Tendons and ligaments of the lower leg*

1. *Tendon sheaths (tendons run through them; contain synovial fluid)*
2. *Check ligament (runs from back of knee to deep digital flexor tendon)*
3. *Superficial flexor tendon (flexes lower leg)*
4. *Deep digital flexor tendon (attaches to bottom of coffin bone beneath navicular bone; flexes lower leg)*
5. *Common digital extensor tendon (down front of leg to coffin bone; extends lower leg)*
6. *Suspensory ligament (from behind metacarpal bones around fetlock joint)*
7. *Branch of suspensory ligament (joins common digital extensor tendon)*
8. *Suspensory band from pastern bone to lateral cartilage*
9. *Digital annular ligament (supports flexor tendons)*

FIGURE 9 *Structures of the lower leg and foot* (continued)

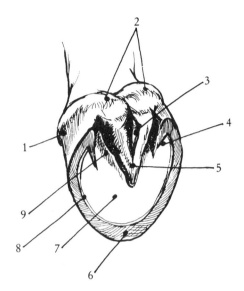
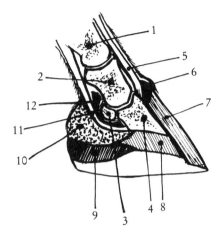

B. *Outer structures of the foot*
   1. *Coronary band*
   2. *Heels*
   3. *Cleft of frog*
   4. *Bars*
   5. *Frog*
   6. *Wall*
   7. *Sole*
   8. *White line*
   9. *Commissures*

C. *Inner structures of the foot*
   1. *Large pastern bone (first phalanx)*
   2. *Small pastern bone (second phalanx)*
   3. *Navicular bone*
   4. *Coffin bone (third phalanx)*
   5. *Common digital extensor tendon (attaches to front of coffin bone)*
   6. *Corium ("nail bed" of laminae and coronary band)*
   7. *Insensitive laminae (of wall)*
   8. *Sensitive liminae (of sole)*
   9. *Frog*
   10. *Digital cushion*
   11. *Deep digital flexor tendon (attaches to underside of coffin bone)*
   12. *Navicular bursa (between navicular bone and tendon)*

3

HOW A HORSE MOVES: THE CYCLE OF MOVEMENT

Movement starts with the desire to go forward. Movement in any gait (trot, canter, etc.) is accomplished stride by stride. A stride is a complete cycle of movement in which all four legs complete their motion and move the whole horse. A step is a movement of one leg. Each leg goes through four phases during a stride: swing, impact, support and thrust.

When the horse starts off from a standstill, it appears that his front legs move first. His thrust actually starts from behind, although his front legs must be picked up and start forward to get out of the way of the hind legs. He is a "rear-engined" animal; he doesn't draw himself along by pulling with his front legs but pushes himself forward with his hind legs. To analyze the cycle of movement that takes place in a stride, it makes sense to begin with the hind legs because that is where the power comes from.

The cycle of movement starts in the hind-quarters. The hind leg is picked up, flexed and brought forward (swing), and then touches the ground (impact). During the support phase the leg bears weight; it is then straightened (extended), and by pushing against the ground (thrust), pushes the horse's body forward by means of the back and trunk. Thrust begins at the moment that the leg is vertical underneath the hindquarter and continues until the foot breaks ground. The leg then flexes and prepares for forward swing again. The horse's head and neck rise, flex, lower and extend in "balancing gestures," which help to shift the center of gravity and to extend and place the forelegs under the center of gravity. At the same time the forelegs are also picked up, flexed, brought forward (swing) and grounded (impact), and support the weight of the forehand, then extend backward against the ground (thrust) until they break over and leave the ground for the next stride. The rhythm, order of

FIGURE 1 *The cycle of movement*

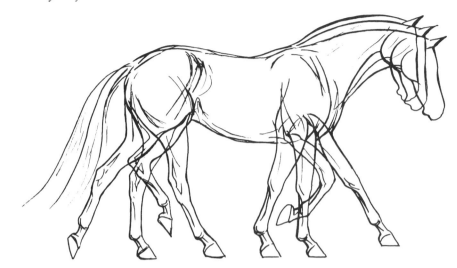

footfalls, posture and technique of using the legs may vary with each gait, but the basic cycle of movement is the same.

The degree to which the hind leg reaches forward under the body is called engagement. The farther the hind leg reaches, the longer the stride and the greater the pushing power. A short, lazy or restricted stride that does not reach very far under the body has little engagement and thus lacks power. The horse can engage his hind legs by swinging each hind leg forward with a fairly straight leg (usually seen in horses that move long and low), or by flexing his loin and tucking his hindquarters underneath him with more flexion in the joints of the hind legs and shorter, higher strides (seen in collected horses that "sit" on their hindquarters). "Swinging" engagement is associated with long strides,

"pushing" power and ground-covering gaits; it tends to go with a more forward balance. "Tucking" engagement of the hindquarters, or "carrying" power, is associated with collected balance, spring and maneuverability, with the horse "working off his hindquarters."

When moving forward, the horse uses the "circle of muscles"—a series of muscle groups that act together and in sequence to make each stride. In a good athlete, these muscles work in harmony, contracting and relaxing in a regular rhythm. No muscle or muscle group is neglected or overstressed, and the muscles become fit and evenly developed through good movement. Poor movement, whether caused by poor conformation, weakness, unsoundness or bad riding and training, overstresses some muscles and un-

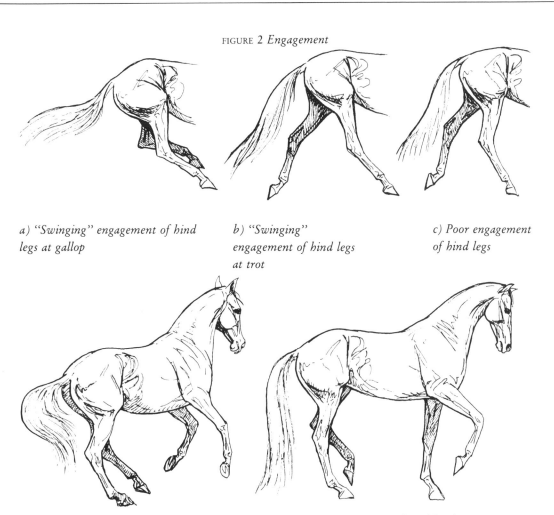

FIGURE 2 *Engagement*

a) "Swinging" engagement of hind legs at gallop

b) "Swinging" engagement of hind legs at trot

c) Poor engagement of hind legs

d) "Tucking" engagement of hindquarters in hindquarter turn

e) "Tucking" engagement of hindquarters in piaffe

derutilizes others, leading to soreness, disability and uneven muscle development. The horse's stance and muscle development are clues to the way he habitually moves and uses (or misuses) his circle of muscles, and how he has been ridden and trained.

When the horse moves in any gait, he uses every muscle in his body. Some muscles have several roles. It is misleading to isolate just one muscle (for instance, to say "The hind leg is brought forward by the iliopsoas muscle"), because many muscles combine to bring

FIGURE 3

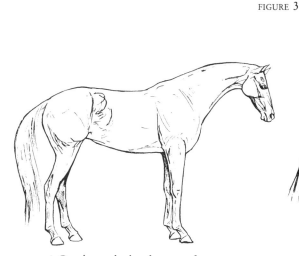

a) Good muscle development from correct movement

b) Incorrect muscle development from poor movement

the hind leg forward, and the iliopsoas muscle has other functions, too. However, to keep this discussion simple, we will look at only a few of the major muscles and structures used in the cycle of movement and describe only their primary role in moving the horse. A complete description of the biomechanics of the horse could fill a whole book!

The muscles of the hindquarters provide the horse's pushing power. The muscles that run from hip to stifle and those at the front of the gaskin (especially the quadriceps group and the vastus muscle) flex the hind leg and bring it forward. The iliopsoas muscle, which runs from the underside of the lumbar vertebrae and the floor of the pelvis to the femurs (thighbones), is important in drawing the hind leg forward and in flexing the loin

(the lumbosacral joint). These muscles play a major role in the engagement of the hind legs. The muscles that run around the back of the hindquarters (especially the hamstring group and the gluteals), straighten the hind leg and push against the ground to move the whole horse forward. They are some of the most powerful muscles in the body.

At every stride, the horses's loins flex (round upward) as the hind legs are engaged under the body. This flexion takes place mostly at the lumbosacral joint, where the pelvis and sacrum (croup) join the last lumbar (lower back) vertebra. This is a key joint in the body, one that allows the hindquarters to tuck under and engage for power, balance and long strides. The psoas group (including the iliopsoas) and the abdominal muscles (es-

FIGURE 4 *Phases of the stride*

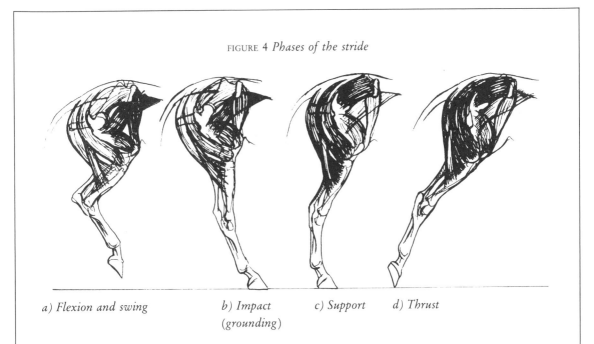

a) *Flexion and swing*   b) *Impact*   c) *Support*   d) *Thrust*
                              (grounding)

pecially the rectus abdominus, which runs from the end of the breastbone to the floor of the pelvis) are the major muscles that flex the loin and engage the hindquarters. The horse's back and loin are not nearly as flexible as those of the dog or cat, which can flex their entire backs enough to get their hind feet in front of the forelegs at each gallop stride. Were a horse that flexible, he could hardly carry a rider on his back!

The horse's loin flexes most at the gallop, when engaging the hind legs for a major effort such as a jump or buck and when he "works off his hindquarters" in collected gaits, sliding stops or transitions. It is an important link in the transmission of power from the hind legs to the rest of the body and allows the horse to balance himself on his

hindquarters when he needs to. A horse that moves with a stiff back, with little flexion in the lumbosacral joint, is handicapped in his ability to move powerfully and to shift his balance.

The hindquarters push the horse forward by means of the spine and the back muscles. The back is something like the drive shaft of a car, which transmits the pushing power of the rear wheels to the rest of the vehicle. However, the horse's back muscles work alternately as he strides with one hind leg and then the other. Each side of the back rounds and rises as the hind leg on that side is engaged and grounded, and it dips as the leg stretches out behind and then is carried forward through the air. This alternating upward movement is easy to see if you watch

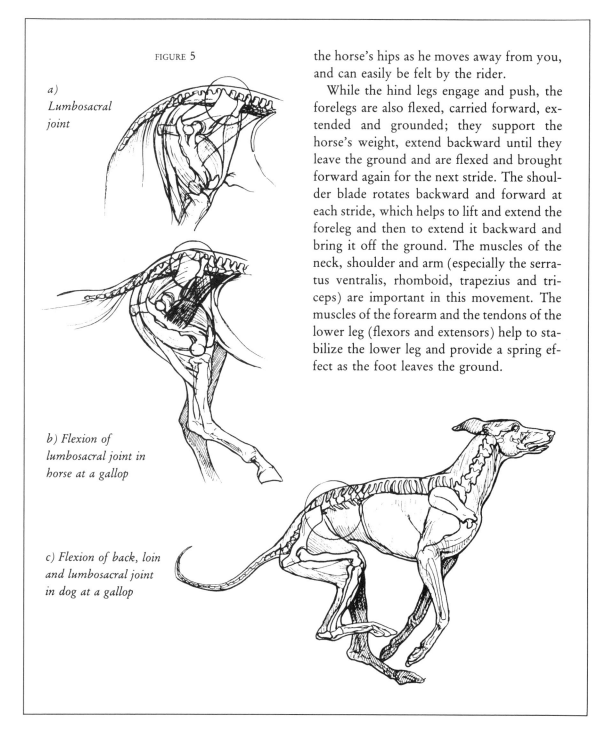

FIGURE 5

a)
*Lumbosacral
joint*

*b) Flexion of
lumbosacral joint in
horse at a gallop*

*c) Flexion of back, loin
and lumbosacral joint
in dog at a gallop*

the horse's hips as he moves away from you, and can easily be felt by the rider.

While the hind legs engage and push, the forelegs are also flexed, carried forward, extended and grounded; they support the horse's weight, extend backward until they leave the ground and are flexed and brought forward again for the next stride. The shoulder blade rotates backward and forward at each stride, which helps to lift and extend the foreleg and then to extend it backward and bring it off the ground. The muscles of the neck, shoulder and arm (especially the serratus ventralis, rhomboid, trapezius and triceps) are important in this movement. The muscles of the forearm and the tendons of the lower leg (flexors and extensors) help to stabilize the lower leg and provide a spring effect as the foot leaves the ground.

FIGURE 6

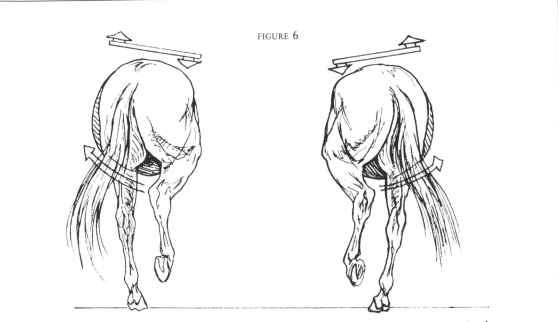

Alternate lift of hips during movement.   *Belly swings out over supporting leg.*

The abdominal muscles (especially the rectus abdominus, a wide sheet of muscle running from breastbone to pelvis) support the internal organs and aid in breathing and other bodily functions. While the abdominals help in rounding the back, it is mainly the psoas group (which lies underneath the lumbar vertebrae) that rounds the back, flexes the loin and draws the hindquarters under the body. Holding the abdominal muscles tightly contracted for too long would interfere with breathing. However, the rectus abdominus does play a greater role in rounding the back and flexing the loin at each stride in the gallop, as the horse breathes in rhythm with each gallop stride. Horses that work at the gallop a lot have strong abdominal muscles and a lean, tucked-up belly.

The rounding of the back in motion is called bascule; it is especially evident over a jump or when the horse moves in true collection. Most of the rounding of the back in bascule takes place at the lumbosacral joint. The horse can round his back in a bascule only when his back muscles are relaxed—it is the psoas and abdominal muscles that round the back. Tense or contracted back muscles will hollow the back and drop the belly instead. Rounding the back in a bascule gives the horse poise, balance and an elastic back mechanism.

The horse's head and neck are his "balancer." Because the horse's head is a heavy weight at the end of a long, flexible neck, the posture in which he carries his neck and any "balancing gestures" he makes by raising,

FIGURE 7

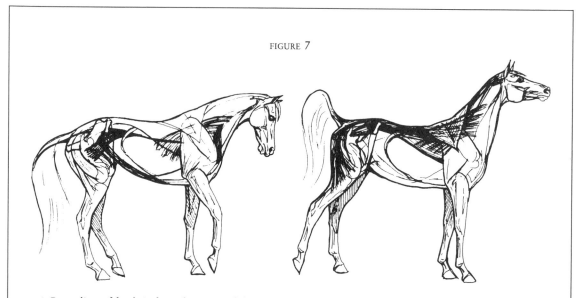

a) Rounding of back in bascule, using abdominal muscles

b) Contracting back muscles causes stiff, hollow back.

flexing, extending or lowering his head and neck can change his entire body balance. A chain of muscles (including the longissimus dorsi, spinalis dorsi, trapezius and rhomboid) interconnect from the croup to the poll. These muscles, along with the dorsal ligaments and the cervical (nuchal) ligament, help connect the back and neck to the hindquarters and are involved in making balancing gestures.

Besides affecting the horse's balance and posture, head and neck movements are important for vision. The horse must raise or lower his head in order to change his focus, so freedom to use his head and neck as he needs to is essential.

The long muscles of the underside of the neck (sternocephalic and brachiocephalic)

help to lower the horse's head, flex the neck and extend the forelegs. The scalenius muscle (a muscle hidden deep in the base of the neck, running from the first rib to the top of the lower cervical vertebrae) helps the serratus ventralis muscle (the shoulder sling) in raising the rib cage and the withers; it also helps the horse to arch and flex his neck at the base of the neck. This neck-telescoping gesture raises and lightens the forehand and is one of the key elements of collection. The serratus ventralis muscle also helps to turn the neck, as does the splenius.

The muscles of the jaw and poll are also important in the circle of muscles, as they can help or hinder the suppleness of the poll (the atlas joint) and the horse's response to the bit

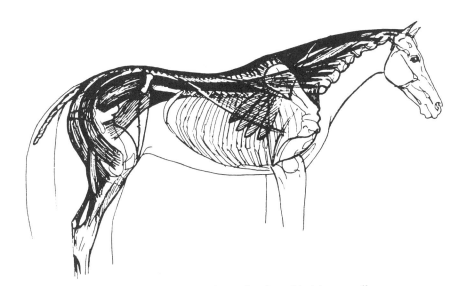

FIGURE 8 *The "chain of muscle" from hind leg to poll*

when ridden. The sternohyoid and omohyoid muscles run from the base of the tongue (at the hyoid bone) to the breastbone and base of the neck. The sternomandibular muscle is a long, slender muscle that runs from the breastbone to the mandible (lower jaw), connecting the mouth to the neck and breast. These muscles, along with the muscles that attach to the poll and atlas (first cervical vertebra) can be elastic and relaxed, which produces a soft, responsive mouth and a balanced head carriage, or they can be stiffly set, usually because of tension due to the rider's bad hands or forcible training methods. When the poll and jaw are relaxed and supple, the horse chews the bit softly with a closed mouth. This relaxes and opens the salivary glands, producing saliva, which turns to foam from the gentle chewing. A rigidly clamped mouth is a "dry" mouth, which is stiff, unyielding and unresponsive. It is also misery to the horse!

The short extrinsic muscles of the poll connect the skull to the atlas and axis (the first two bones of the neck). When these muscles are relaxed and supple, they allow the horse to carry his head in a soft and flexible attitude that makes it easy for him to respond to the rider's hands. Rigid, tight poll muscles create a stiff poll, which goes with discomfort and resistance.

When studying movement, it is important to notice how the horse uses his entire circle of muscles. In good movement, all the major muscle groups work in harmony and the circle of muscles is engaged. Poor movement leaves some muscles disengaged and overstresses others.

FIGURE 9 *a) Neck telescoping gesture, raising the base of the neck*

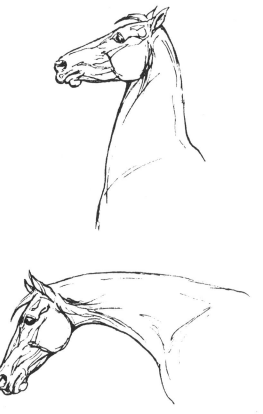

b), c) Balancing gestures of the head and neck

Although it looks and feels as if the horse can bend his spine evenly from poll to tail in a turn, this is not what actually happens during lateral flexion, or bending. The neck and tail are very flexible, but very little lateral bending can take place in the thoracic (back and ribs) and lumbar spine because of the shapes of the vertebrae and the way they articulate with each other, and the sacrum cannot bend sideways at all. The muscles that run along the side of the rib cage (especially the external oblique) can contract on one side, bending the trunk laterally a little. However, the spine actually lifts and rotates as much as it bends laterally in turning, at least from the withers back.

The neck, of course, is very flexible and can allow the horse to reach all the way back to his flank with his head. This movement is made partly by contracting the muscles on one side of the trunk and partly by contracting the muscles along the side of the neck, especially the serratus ventralis muscles.

Lateral (sideways) movement is not part of the ordinary forward stride, but horses can turn, pivot, dodge or move sideways quickly and easily. The forelegs can be spread, tilted to the side, swung inward and even crossed

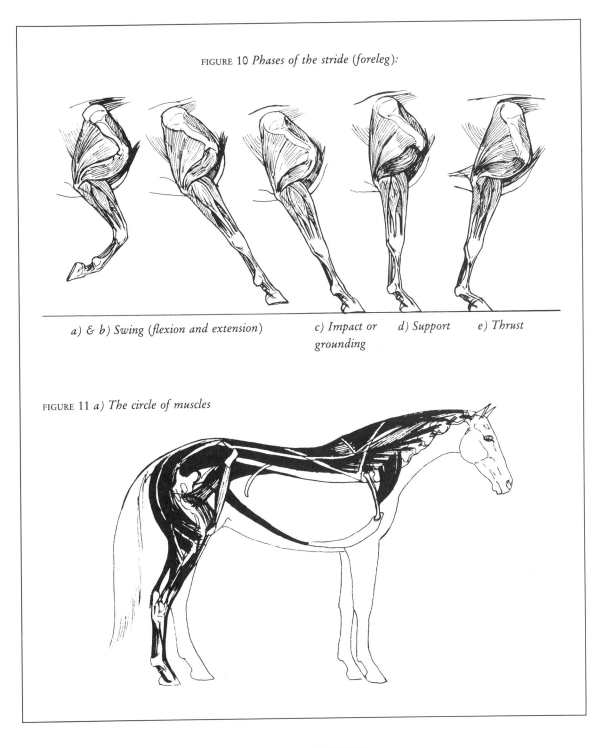

FIGURE 10 *Phases of the stride (foreleg):*

a) & b) Swing (flexion and extension)   *c) Impact or grounding*   *d) Support*   *e) Thrust*

FIGURE 11 *a) The circle of muscles*

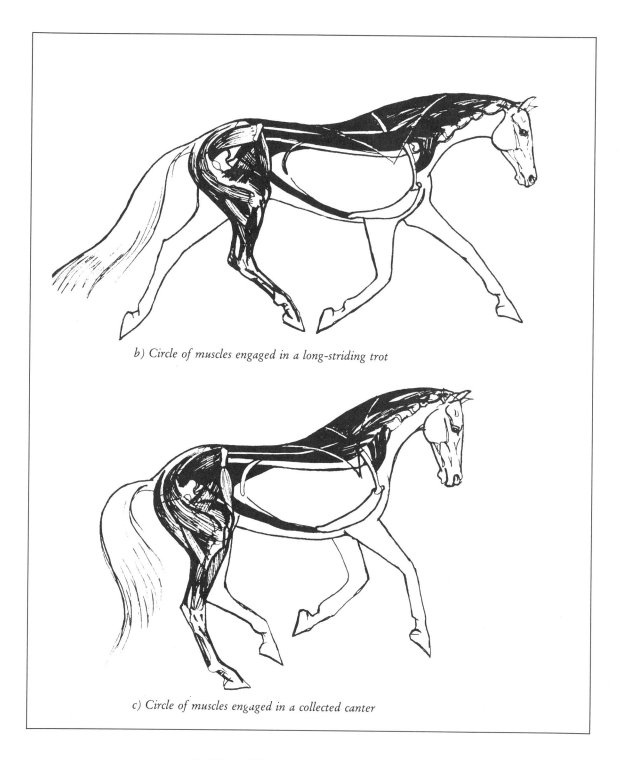

b) Circle of muscles engaged in a long-striding trot

c) Circle of muscles engaged in a collected canter

FIGURE 12 *The muscles of the shoulder sling:*

1. *Rhomboid*
2. *Trapezius*
3. *Thoracic part of serratus ventralis*
4. *Anterior deep pectoral*
5. *Posterior deep pectoral*
6. *Superficial pectoral*

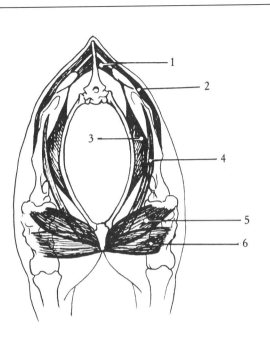

for lateral balance and movement. The hind legs can also be abducted (moved outward) and adducted (moved inward). The joints of the legs are not constructed to allow very much sideways movement in the stifle, hock, elbow, knee or fetlock joints, so most lateral leg movement begins high up at the top of the leg.

In the forelegs, the muscles at the inside and top of the shoulder blade (chiefly the trapezius and rhomboid muscles) can tilt the shoulder blade, causing the foreleg to reach outward (abduction). The pectoral muscles, which run from the breastbone to the forearm, bring the foreleg inward (adduction). To move sideways easily, the horse must free the forehand by shifting his weight back somewhat, onto the hindquarters.

In the hind leg, the large muscles on the outside of the thigh, especially the gluteals and rectus femoris muscles, are used for abduction, or outward movement of the leg. The inner muscles of the hindquarters and inner gaskins (gracilis and adductor femoris) bring the hind leg inward (adduction).

4

THE GAITS AND
TRANSITIONS

The horse's gaits or paces are his natural ways of moving. The walk, trot and gallop are the natural gaits common to most equines, including horses, asses and zebras; some have a hereditary tendency to pace instead of trot. Other gaits such as the canter, the stepping pace and the rack are refined from the basic natural gaits by training. Some, like the running walk and the paso gait, require an inborn affinity for the gait that is part of the heritage of certain breeds.

Any gait can be performed well or badly. A "pure" gait is one that is performed fluently with a true, clean rhythm, moving freely and without mistakes or constraint. *Irregular,* or *"impure,"* gaits under saddle may be caused by lameness or unsoundness or, more often, by the interference of the rider, especially in his use of the bridle. This may be a momentary and incidental mistake, or it can become an habitual pattern that eventually ruins the horse's natural gaits. Irregular and incorrect gaits are always less efficient than pure gaits and go with a distorted balance and way of using the body. They may point to poor riding, poor training or unsoundness, and may lead to unsoundness.

THE WALK

The walk is a four-beat gait, executed in four-time. Four distinct hoofbeats are heard as each foot in succession strikes the ground. Two or three legs are always on the ground, making the walk the most stable of the gaits and the easiest to ride.

The sequence of the walk is (1) left hind, (2) left fore, (3) right hind, (4) right fore. (When a horse begins walking from the halt, it appears that one foreleg moves first. However, since the power comes from the hindquarters, the walk sequence is said to start with a hind leg.)

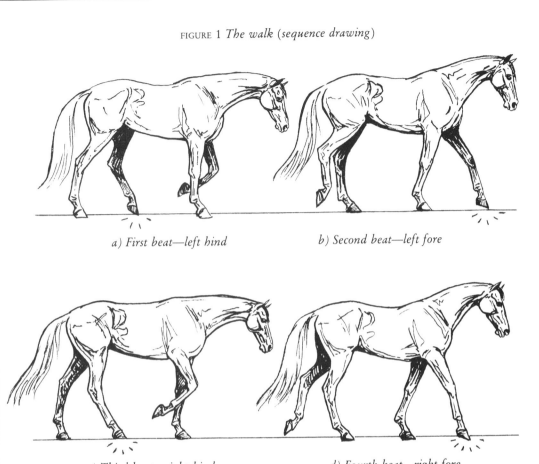

FIGURE 1 *The walk (sequence drawing)*

a) First beat—left hind

b) Second beat—left fore

c) Third beat—right hind

d) Fourth beat—right fore

The four beats should be clear, distinct and evenly spaced, without shuffling, quickening or altering the rhythm.

The speed of the ordinary walk is approximately 4 miles per hour.

In a good walk, the horse moves with a swinging back and good engagement, which causes him to put down each hind foot a little beyond the track left by the front foot on that side. This is called overstepping or over-tracking. A good walker will also make generous balancing gestures with his head and neck and will allow his tail to swing freely with each stride.

Types of Walk

ORDINARY WALK   An average walk of about 4 mph, with good engagement and moderate overstep. Also called the working walk.

FREE WALK   A walk of relaxation, in which the horse reaches forward with long strides and a relaxed back and lowered neck. May be ridden on loose reins or on a long rein.

COLLECTED WALK   An energetic, elastic marching gait with a regular four-beat rhythm. The horse remains on the bit with neck raised and arched, head near the vertical, hindquarters well engaged, and shorter, higher and active steps. Because the steps are shorter, he does not overstep.

EXTENDED WALK   A walk in which the horse covers as much ground as possible at each stride without quickening his tempo or losing his clear, regular four-beat rhythm. He reaches well forward from the hips and shoulders, and his head and neck extend forward. His hind feet overstep well beyond the prints of the front feet.

MEDIUM WALK   A walk of moderate extension, performed on the bit. It is required of medium- to advanced-level dressage horses.

The walk has been called the easiest gait to ruin and the most difficult gait to repair. This is because tension caused by forced training is apt to show up in a faulty walk; the bad habit may return in moments of stress long after the trainer thinks he has conquered the problem.

FIGURE 1-B *Types of walk:*

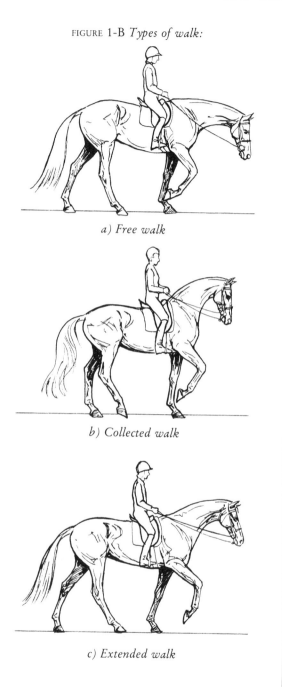

a) Free walk

b) Collected walk

c) Extended walk

Faults in the Walk

JIGGING Describes the irregular, tense jog trot a horse performs instead of walking. Difficult to control and uncomfortable to ride, it often occurs when a horse is anxious to catch up with horses ahead of him or to get back to the barn.

LAZY WALK A toe-dragging walk that lacks engagement, balance and forward swing.

IRREGULAR PACING WALK A walk in which both legs on one side move forward nearly together, with the four-beat rhythm almost becoming two beats. This is caused by tension and stiffness, particularly in the back and neck, and is sometimes seen in horses that have been forced into difficult movements before they are ready. It a serious fault because it is awkward and particularly hard to cure.

THE TROT

The trot is a two-beat diagonal gait with suspension, executed in two-time. This means that the diagonal pairs of feet strike the ground together for one hoofbeat, then the horse pushes off and is suspended in the air for a moment before the opposite diagonal pair of feet strike for the second beat. The sequence is (1) right hind and left fore (suspension), (2) left hind and right fore (suspension). The moment of suspension gives the trot its characteristic spring or bounce.

The trot should always have two clean

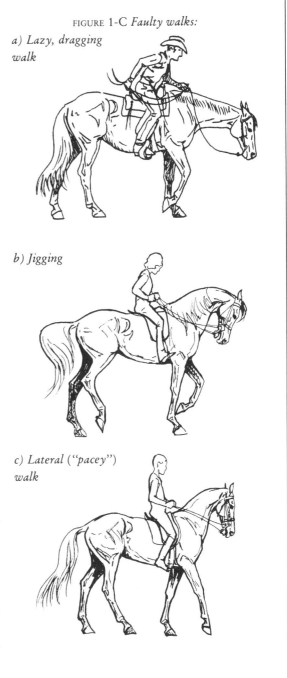

FIGURE 1-C *Faulty walks:*

a) Lazy, dragging walk

b) Jigging

c) Lateral ("pacey") walk

FIGURE 2 *The trot (sequence)*

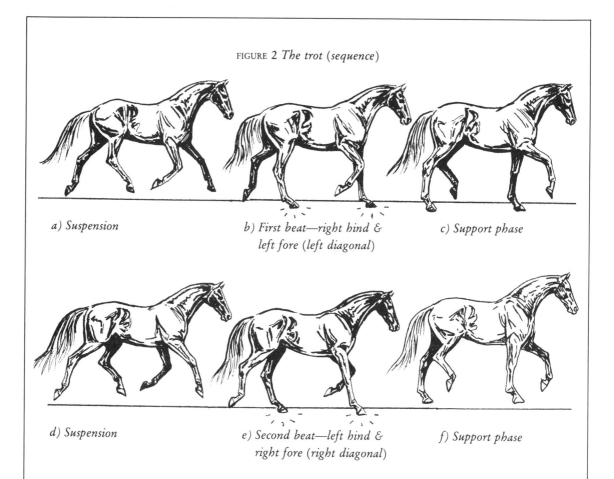

a) *Suspension*

b) *First beat—right hind & left fore (left diagonal)*

c) *Support phase*

d) *Suspension*

e) *Second beat—left hind & right fore (right diagonal)*

f) *Support phase*

beats, with a regular, even rhythm and tempo. There should be no extra beats, shuffling or loss of suspension. The diagonal legs should move in unison, with the front and hind cannons parallel as they are brought forward. A good trot has engagement, with springy, round and relaxed back muscles. The moment of suspension is longest in the extended trot and shorter in the collected or shortened trot, but it should never be lost entirely. The tempo should remain the same

even when the horse lengthens or shortens his strides; it should not quicken or slow.

The speed of the ordinary trot averages between 6 and 8 miles per hour. A racing Standardbred may reach a top speed of up to 30 mph.

When a rider posts, or rises to the trot, he sits and rises with one diagonal pair of legs. This diagonal is named for the foreleg—i.e., if he posts with the left front leg and the right hind leg, he is said to be posting on the left

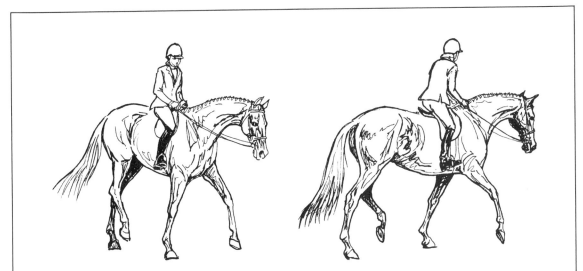

FIGURE 3 *Posting on the outside diagonal. Rider sits and rises with the outside foreleg and inside hind leg on a turn.*

diagonal. In North America it is customary to post on the outside diagonal (when riding to the right, on the left diagonal). This makes it easier for the inside hind leg to engage well during a turn. The rider should change diagonals whenever he changes direction. Posting on one diagonal without ever changing puts more stress on those legs and can lead to the horse becoming one-sided.

Types of Trot

WORKING TROT   A gait in which the average horse is properly balanced and goes forward with elasticity, good rhythm and impulsion. The hind feet step into the tracks left by the front feet. The working trot is slightly collected; it is a gait between the collected trot and the medium trot. It is used by young horses not yet trained and ready for a fully collected trot.

COLLECTED TROT   A shorter, elastic and energetic trot with the horse's balance shifted backward. The horse remains on the bit and moves with well-engaged hindquarters, shorter and higher steps and a rounded back, with his neck raised and arched and his face near the vertical. The tempo should remain the same—it must not become slower.

MEDIUM TROT   A "big" trot performed with a round outline, with great impulsion from the hindquarters and moderately extended steps. It is a gait between the working trot and the extended trot, required of medium- to high-level dressage horses.

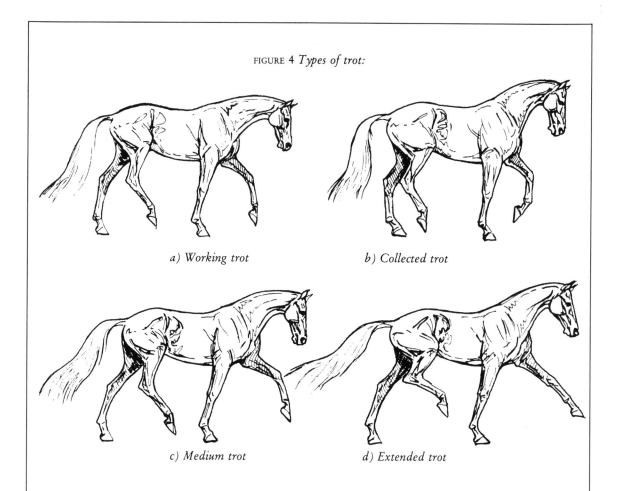

FIGURE 4 *Types of trot:*

a) *Working trot*

b) *Collected trot*

c) *Medium trot*

d) *Extended trot*

EXTENDED TROT A gait in which the horse covers as much ground as possible with each stride. The horse pushes off the ground with great impulsion, allowing for the greatest possible reach, suspension and lengthening of his stride while remaining in balance. He must remain on the bit without leaning on it, and must not quicken his tempo; the diagonal pairs of legs must remain united and the forefeet should touch the ground at the spot toward which they are pointing.

JOG TROT A relaxed, shortened trot with minimum suspension, usually performed on a loose rein. The horse's back should be elastic, the diagonals clear and the rhythm regular. The jog is the easiest trot to ride because it has little suspension. It should remain a clean, two-beat gait without shuffling or breaking up the diagonal rhythm. Western horses are ridden at a jog; it is a comfortable gait for both horse and rider over long distances.

FIGURE 5 *Types of trot:*

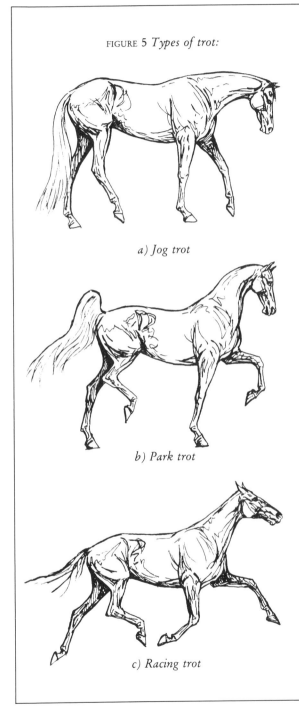

a) *Jog trot*

b) *Park trot*

c) *Racing trot*

PARK TROT A balanced, showy trot with collection and high action, performed by gaited Saddle Horses and Park horses. The forelegs are flexed and raised until the forearm is horizontal or higher. The action should be balanced, with the hind legs as active and flexed as much as the forelegs.

RACING TROT A trot extended to the maximum. The diagonal pair may begin to separate, with the hind leg grounding first. The head and neck are high and extended. This trot is seen in racing Standardbreds—it should not be confused with the extended trot normally expected of riding horses.

PASSAGE A highly collected, very elevated and cadenced trot with tremendous energy. The horse raises each diagonal high off the ground and remains suspended in the air for a longer period between hoofbeats. The hindquarters are more engaged than in other trots, and the hocks and knees are flexed more, producing a brilliant trot in which the horse appears to dance in slow motion. The passage is performed at the highest levels of dressage.

PIAFFE A highly collected and cadenced trot performed nearly in place with suspension and a clear rhythm. The hindquarters are well engaged and slightly lowered, and the hind legs bend more in all their joints; the forehand and shoulders are light and free, with more flexion in the forelegs. Like the passage, the piaffe belongs to the highest levels of dressage.

FIGURE 5-A *Highly balanced modes of trot:*

a) Piaffe   *b) Passage*

Faulty trots usually result from poor balance or from attempting to adjust the horse's trot by making it move faster or slower than its best working tempo. Asking for more collection or greater extension than the horse is able to produce at his stage of training can cause a horse to develop distorted and irregular gaits. Bad riding, especially misusing the bridle, can produce "bridle lameness"—a rhythmic, one-sided resistance that resembles the bobbing head of a lame horse, which is very difficult to eradicate.

Faults in the Trot

STIFF, HOLLOW TROT   Stiffness and tension cause the back muscles to "lock up" rather than produce elastic swinging. The back is hollow and the head is carried high and stiffly. This causes a rough gait that is very uncomfortable for both horse and rider and may lead to a sore back in the horse and overstressed legs and joints.

LOSS OF SUSPENSION (STEPPING) IN JOG   The horse loses the spring and suspension and simply steps from one diagonal to the other. This is often seen in western horses that are made to jog slower than they can jog correctly. It is easier to ride than a too-fast jog, but can easily become stiff and "peggy" or break into a walk.

FALSE   EXTENSION   Also   called   goose-stepping and toe-flipping. The horse hyperextends his forelegs so that the toes flip up in an exaggerated manner. The foreleg must be retracted slightly before it can touch the ground. While this action is spectacular, it is a sign of tension, constraint and stiffness instead of true extension. The horse "promises more in front than he delivers behind"; the

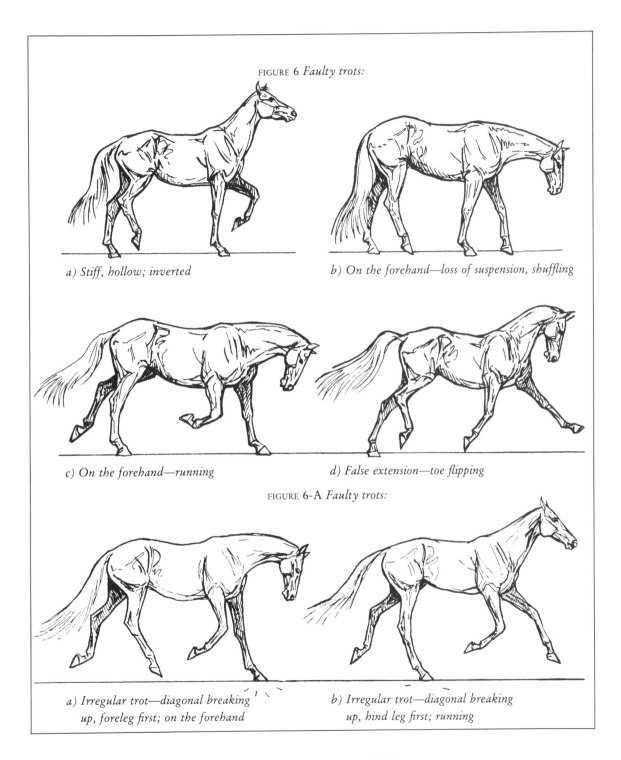

FIGURE 6 *Faulty trots:*

a) Stiff, hollow; inverted

b) On the forehand—loss of suspension, shuffling

c) On the forehand—running

d) False extension—toe flipping

FIGURE 6-A *Faulty trots:*

*a) Irregular trot—diagonal breaking
up, foreleg first; on the forehand*

*b) Irregular trot—diagonal breaking
up, hind leg first; running*

engagement and impulsion from the hind legs are insufficient. This fault is often seen in dressage horses that are driven strongly forward against a forcibly restraining hand.

GOING WIDE BEHIND (STRADDLING)   Seen in a faulty extended trot when the horse cannot handle his balance with that length of stride. The hind legs go wide apart instead of reaching forward under the center of gravity, which is a sign that the horse is past his limit in extension.

IRREGULAR TROT, FORE FOOT FIRST   The horse is on the forehand; the hind leg is not engaged enough, so the foreleg lands first instead of a true diagonal beat. This fault is often seen when the horse is lazy, lacking impulsion, or has been forced to trot or jog too slowly for his balance and coordination. It resembles "trotting in front and walking behind," which is a common fault in western pleasure horses.

IRREGULAR TROT, HIND FOOT FIRST   The horse is "strung out" and running with an irregular rhythm; the hind leg lands first instead of a true diagonal beat. This is common in racing Standardbreds at top speed; in a riding horse, it is a sign that the trot has been pushed past the limits of balance and coordination.

THE CANTER

The canter is a three-beat gait with suspension, performed in a three-time rhythm. It is a series of "jumps," or bounds, with suspension between strides. The sequence of the gait is (1) outside hind leg (first beat), (2) diagonal pair of legs (second beat), (3) inside foreleg (third beat), followed by suspension.

One side is said to be the lead or leading leg. In a left lead canter, the sequence of the gait is (1) right hind, (2) left hind and right fore (diagonal pair), (3) left fore, or leading foreleg (suspension). In a right lead canter, the sequence is: (1) left hind, (2) right hind and left fore (diagonal pair), (3) right fore, or leading foreleg (suspension).

The horse should normally lead with the inside legs; i.e., when turning left, he should be on the left lead. Cantering with the outside legs leading by mistake is unhandy and makes it difficult to balance in a turn. This is called a wrong lead or false lead.

The transition into the canter is called a canter depart. When the horse changes direction in the canter, he may change leads with a flying change by switching leads within a single canter stride, or he may break to a trot and resume the canter on the new lead. This is called changing leads through the trot. In a simple change of lead, the horse breaks to a walk for one or two strides between leads.

A good canter is regular, light and active, with an elastic back, good balance and three clean beats in a steady rhythm, on the correct lead. It is somewhat more collected than the gallop. The horse moves straight, with his

FIGURE 7 *The canter (left lead) (sequence):*

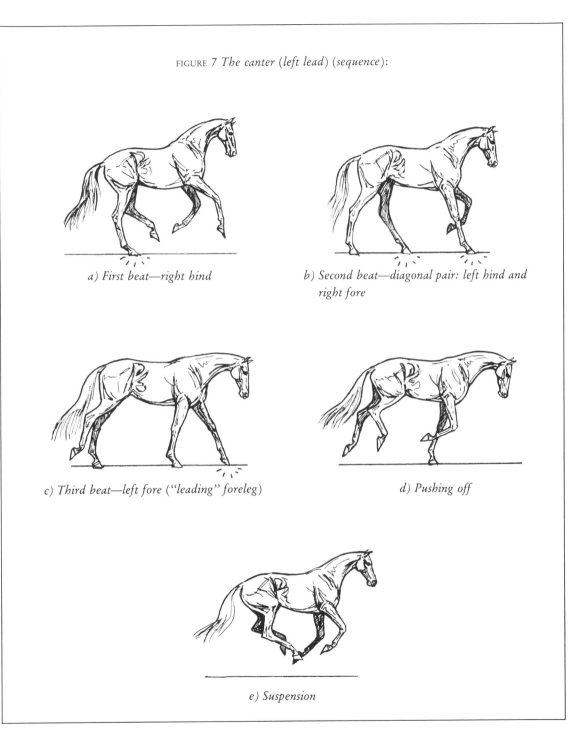

a) First beat—right hind

b) Second beat—diagonal pair: left hind and right fore

c) Third beat—left fore ("leading" foreleg)

d) Pushing off

e) Suspension

FIGURE 8 *Leads at the canter:*

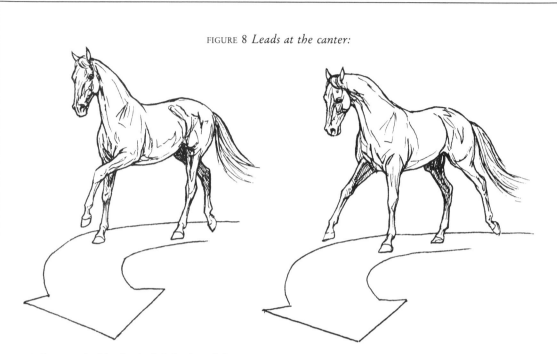

a) Correct (inside) lead—left lead on left turn

b) Incorrect (outside) lead—right lead on left turn

hind legs tracking his forelegs, and not crooked or slightly sideways. The canter has a gentle rocking motion that makes it one of the most pleasant gaits for the rider.

Types of Canter

WORKING CANTER The horse canters in good balance, somewhat collected, with even, light and cadenced strides and good impulsion. He is elastic and on the bit, but does not show as much collection as required for a fully collected canter. The working canter is performed by horses that are not yet trained and ready for collected movements. It is used for ordinary canter work and jumping.

COLLECTED CANTER The horse moves forward with light, elastic and shortened strides and on the bit, with hindquarters well engaged. The balance is shifted backward and the back is rounded, with the neck raised and arched and the face near the vertical. The strides are shorter and higher, with supple, free and active shoulders and much impulsion from the hindquarters. The rhythm and tempo must remain the same as the horse collects his canter. The collected canter is performed by English pleasure horses, Park horses and other show horses as well as medium to advanced dressage horses.

MEDIUM CANTER   A bigger, "rounder" canter, between the working canter and extended canter. The horse goes forward with free, balanced and moderately extended strides, remaining in balance and rhythm. The medium canter is required of medium to advanced dressage horses.

EXTENDED CANTER   The horse covers the most ground possible with each stride, while remaining in a balanced, light, three-beat canter. His neck and head extend somewhat forward and he remains on the bit without leaning. He does not speed up his tempo or change to a gallop rhythm. The extended canter is required of medium to advanced dressage horses.

COUNTER-CANTER   Cantering on the outside lead on purpose, as a training and suppling exercise. It should not be confused with an accidental wrong lead!

LOPE   A relaxed, unconstrained canter usually performed on a loose rein. The horse remains in a true three-beat canter with suspension, but his frame is longer, and his neck is carried lower than in the collected canter and there is less suspension. The hind legs should be well engaged under the body, and the horse light and well balanced. The lope is used in western riding and is easy on both horse and rider for long-distance riding.

   A good canter requires suppleness, balance and coordination; faulty canters are all too common. Confusion about the signals for the correct lead or the timing of the canter depart

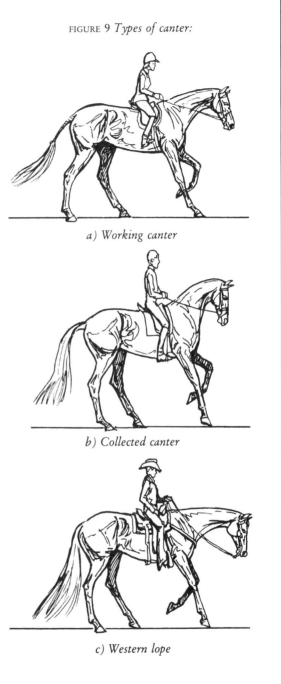

FIGURE 9 *Types of canter:*

a) Working canter

b) Collected canter

c) Western lope

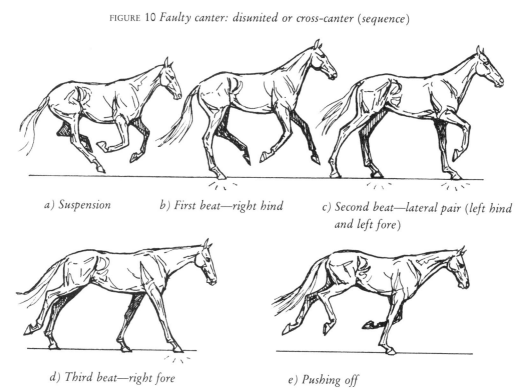

FIGURE 10 *Faulty canter: disunited or cross-canter (sequence)*

a) Suspension   *b) First beat—right hind*   *c) Second beat—lateral pair (left hind and left fore)*

d) Third beat—right fore

e) Pushing off
Horse is on left lead behind and right lead in front.

can result in wrong leads or awkward canter departs; a fumbled canter depart or change of leads can result in a disunited canter, or cross-canter. (The term "cross-firing" is sometimes used incorrectly to describe a cross-canter.) This is an uncoordinated gait in which the horse is on one lead with his hind legs and on the other with his front legs. It has a lateral rolling motion and makes the horse unbalanced and unable to engage his hind legs for safe turning.

Faults in the Canter, or Lope

WRONG LEAD.

DISUNITED CANTER (CROSS-CANTER).

IRREGULAR FOUR-BEAT CANTER, FORELEG FIRST Instead of the diagonal pair of legs striking together, the foreleg strikes first. This occurs when the horse is "strung out" and canters on the forehand. It is a common fault in western pleasure horses that are forced to lope too slowly for their balance and coordination. It resembles "cantering in front and trotting behind."

IRREGULAR FOUR-BEAT CANTER, HIND LEG FIRST   Instead of the diagonal pair of legs striking together, the hind foot strikes first. This often occurs when the horse is forced into a shorter stride and slower canter than he can handle with balance and collection, especially if the rider "pumps" his forehand up and down. It is associated with a stiff, hollow back instead of an elastic, coordinated canter. This fault is often seen in Saddle Seat horses and occasionally in dressage horses that are incorrectly collected.

LATERAL ("PACEY") CANTER   The horse canters with the correct lead and gait sequence, but the left fore and hind legs and the right fore and hind legs move almost together, resembling a pace. There is a distinct lateral movement, and the shoulders may "roll" from side to side. This fault is often seen in horses with a tendency to pace. It is due to stiffness in the back and neck.

THE GALLOP

The gallop is a four-beat gait with suspension, with a leading side, and executed in four-time. It is a series of "jumps" with suspension and is the horse's natural speed gait. The sequence is similar to that of the canter, except that the inside hind leg lands first, instead of a diagonal pair of legs landing together. The sequence of the gallop is:

FIGURE 11 *Faulty canters:*

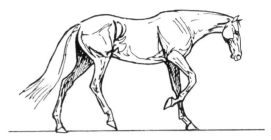

a) Irregular four-beat canter—diagonal breaking up, foreleg first; on the forehand

b) Irregular four-beat canter—diagonal breaking up, hind leg first; pumping

c) Lateral four-beat canter—approaching a pace

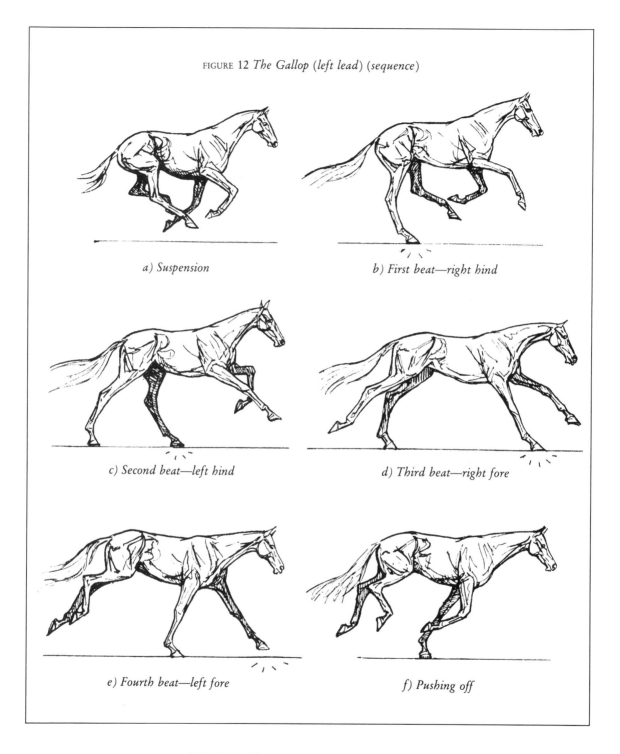

FIGURE 12 *The Gallop (left lead) (sequence)*

a) Suspension

b) First beat—right hind

c) Second beat—left hind

d) Third beat—right fore

e) Fourth beat—left fore

f) Pushing off

(1) outside hind leg, (2) inside hind, (3) outside foreleg, (4) inside (leading) foreleg (suspension).

The sequence of the left lead gallop is (1) right hind, (2) left hind, (3) right fore, (4) left fore (leading foreleg) (suspension). The right lead sequence is (1) left hind, (2) right hind, (3) left fore, (4) right fore (leading foreleg) (suspension).

The gallop is an extended gait, with long strides, great engagement and much flexion (bascule) of the loin at the lumbosacral joint. The horse uses his abdominal muscles to help engage his hind legs at each stride; this makes him breathe in rhythm with the gallop strides. The head and neck oscillate forward and back in large balancing gestures, and the balance is carried forward.

The speed of the gallop varies from about 18 mph (a hand gallop or hunting pace that can be maintained over a long distance) up to 45 mph for a race horse sprinting at top speed.

Types of Gallop

HAND GALLOP   A controlled gallop executed "in hand," about 18 mph. It should be well balanced so that the horse can handle changes in direction or terrain and can jump in stride. It is used when speed, endurance and maneuverability are required.

RACING GALLOP   A more extended gallop, up to top speed; from about 30 to 45 mph. Distance racers and steeplechasers gallop more slowly but with longer strides than sprinters. Even a racing gallop must remain regular and balanced or the horse will not be able to sustain it for very long.

Faults in the gallop are similar to those in the canter. The gallop may be unbalanced, disunited or executed on the wrong lead. Race horses usually change leads late in a race in order to switch to the less tired legs: a fumbled flying change can result in a disunited gallop.

Faults in the Gallop

WRONG LEAD.

DISUNITED GALLOP.

SCRAMBLING   The horse's attempt to save his balance when trying to turn too fast or too tightly at speed. The hind legs make short, "bunny hopping" strides together instead of performing the normal gallop sequence; the inside hind leg is not sufficiently engaged and the horse can easily slip into a disunited gallop. This fault is often seen in barrel racers and jumpers trying to turn at speed against the clock; it costs time and can cause a fall.

THE REIN-BACK (BACKING UP)

Horses seldom back up in nature, and never back up very far; they are more likely to turn around to get out of a tight spot. The rein-back (also called backing up) is a somewhat unnatural movement and is more difficult for the horse than natural forward movements. In backing up, the horse engages his hind legs and moves back in a diagonal pattern. The foreleg is set down slightly before the hind leg, creating four distinct beats. The sequence is (1) right fore, (2) left hind, (3) left fore, (4) right hind.

The horse should back calmly and willingly, flexing softly at the poll and in the mouth. He should be willing to move forward at any time without sticking, or hesitating. Anticipating the rider's request to back and rushing backward are serious faults because they can lead to a loss of control and to rearing or falling over backward. Resistance, freezing in place and refusing to back, or backing stiffly and reluctantly also show a lack of training or cooperation between horse and rider. Other faults in backing include dragging the feet backward without raising them, irregular and not diagonal pattern, hollowing the back and raising the head, dropping behind the bit and backing crookedly.

THE PACE

The pace is a two-beat lateral gait with suspension, performed in two-time. The sequence is (1) left hind and left fore (suspension), (2) right hind and right fore (suspension).

The pace is fast and fairly smooth, although some horses have a distinct side-to-side roll. It is used in harness racing, but is less common as a saddle gait than the four-beat lateral gaits such as the rack, singlefoot and paso. Most horses that pace have an inborn affinity for the gait; they may naturally pace instead of trot.

In pacing, the horse shows more rotation of the spine from side to side and less lateral bending than in the trot. The head and neck are held high and straight and there are no oscillations, or balancing gestures. Harness racing pacers have their heads held high, straight and steady by an overcheck and a head pole to help maintain the head carriage that facilitates speed and steadiness in the pace. They also wear hopples that connect the foreleg and hind leg of the same side to prevent breaking the gait.

The speed of the pace ranges from about 12 mph to more than 30 mph for a racing Standardbred at top speed. It is usually slightly faster than a comparable trot.

THE AMBLE AND ITS DERIVATIVES

The amble is a four-beat lateral gait derived from the pace and performed in four-time. The sequence is the same as the walk, but the rhythm and execution make it closer to the pace. It is performed without suspension, with the horse stepping from one leg to another, which makes it stable and easy to ride. The amble is a very old gait, preferred for long-distance riding from ancient times because it is smooth, comfortable and easy on the horse and the rider. There are many variations of the amble, with most being associ-

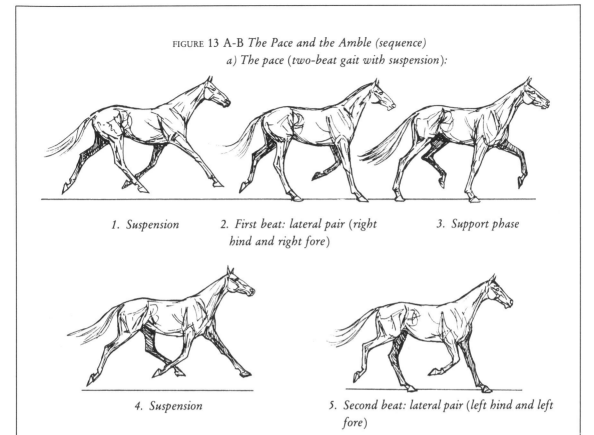

FIGURE 13 A-B *The Pace and the Amble (sequence)*
a) The pace (two-beat gait with suspension):

1. Suspension *2. First beat: lateral pair (right hind and right fore)* *3. Support phase*

4. Suspension *5. Second beat: lateral pair (left hind and left fore)*

ated with a particular breed. Most horses that execute the amble or other four-beat lateral gaits have a natural affinity for the pace or for their breed's particular lateral gait.

The sequence of all four-beat lateral gaits is (1) left hind, (2) left fore, (3) right hind, (4) right fore.

Unlike the true pace, the amble and other four-beat lateral gaits can be collected, which produces the form, balance and ideal style of the various four-beat lateral gaits.

Four-Beat Lateral Gaits

THE RACK, OR SINGLEFOOT Of the four-beat lateral gaits, this gait performed by the five-gaited American Saddle Horse, is the most spectacular. The colloquial name of the gait derives from the fact that the horse at times has only a single foot on the ground (as opposed to the pace, in which he either has two feet on the ground or none at all). This gait must be performed with both speed and form, meaning that the horse must raise his

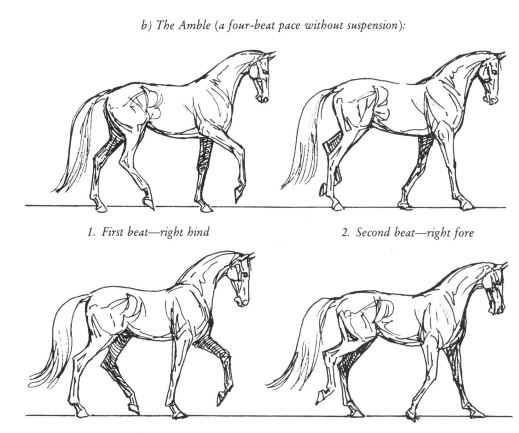

b) The Amble (a four-beat pace without suspension):

1. First beat—right hind

2. Second beat—right fore

3. Third beat—left hind

4. Fourth beat—left fore

hocks and knees high without sacrificing speed in order to do so. The rack requires dynamic impulsion; it is strenuous for the horse but smooth and easy to ride. The hind legs engage well under the body to give the gait its drive and gliding motion, but they are flexed in all their joints for high action. The rhythm is a marked, regular four-time. The rack is executed from the slow gait by extending the gait.

Faulty performance at the rack includes lack of speed, low action, loss of balance and irregular form, lugging on the bit (a sign of insufficient collection), and hitching, sprawling or breaking gait. The rack must never degenerate into a pace. In order to rack well, a horse must have his hocks well engaged and must be light on the forehand. Hesitating, "choking up" and reluctance to move out at speed when called upon are major faults in the rack.

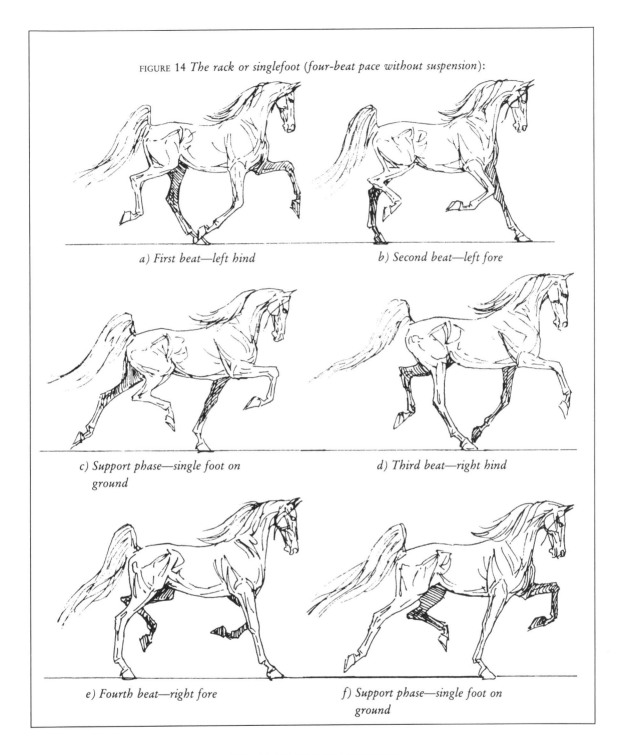

FIGURE 14 *The rack or singlefoot (four-beat pace without suspension):*

a) *First beat—left hind*

b) *Second beat—left fore*

c) *Support phase—single foot on ground*

d) *Third beat—right hind*

e) *Fourth beat—right fore*

f) *Support phase—single foot on ground*

THE GAITS AND TRANSITIONS

53

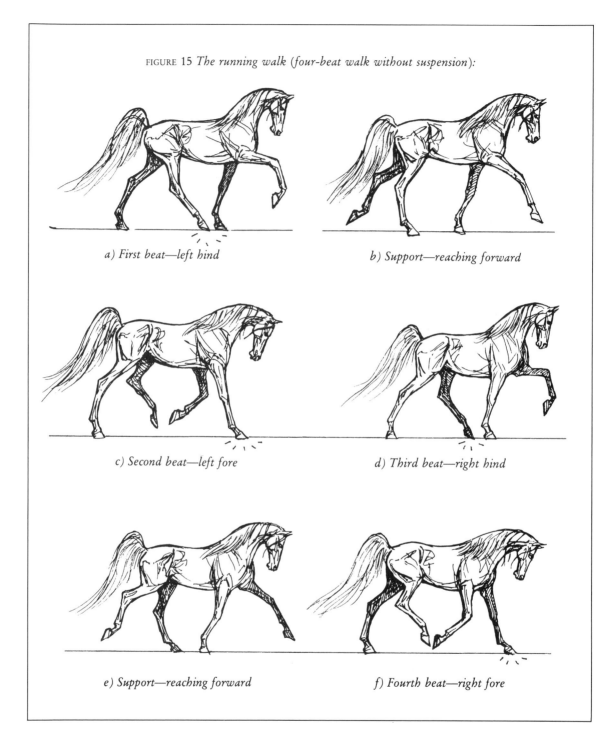

FIGURE 15 *The running walk (four-beat walk without suspension):*

a) First beat—left hind

b) Support—reaching forward

c) Second beat—left fore

d) Third beat—right hind

e) Support—reaching forward

f) Fourth beat—right fore

THE SLOW GAIT, OR STEPPING PACE   A collected form of the rack, performed by the five-gaited American Saddle Horse. The horse must maintain a clear four-time rhythm with evenly spaced beats and great impulsion, in good form (high action in front and hind legs), and should not lunge into a rack prematurely or show any tendency to pace or break his gait. The same faults described in the rack would be detrimental in the slow gait.

THE TØLT   A natural rack performed by Icelandic horses. The head and neck are held high, with less flexion at the poll and arching of the neck than is common in American Saddle Horses.

THE RUNNING WALK   The characteristic gait of the Tennessee Walking Horse. The gait pattern is the same as the ordinary walk, or flat walk, but it is executed with a special technique that gives it a unique gliding quality and makes it extremely smooth. The hind legs engage far under the body with a reaching, gliding step and with less hock flexion than in the rack or slow gait. The horse moves in a croup-low position with much flexion in the lumbosacral joint, which allows maximum engagement; the hind foot oversteps far beyond the print of the forefoot, sometimes as much as 24 inches. The forelegs reach far up and forward with each stride, and there is a characteristic nodding of the head with the rhythm. There is no suspension, nor does the horse "single-foot" as in the rack. The speed varies from 10 or 12 mph to over 20 mph. A tendency to pace or trot is considered a serious fault.

THE PASO GAITS   The paso is a collected amble performed by Paso Fino and Peruvian Paso horses. It is a four-beat lateral gait with balance, moderately high action and clearly marked rhythm. Variations of the paso are the paso fino, paso corto and paso largo (collected, medium and extended forms). Peruvian Paso horses exhibit a characteristic called "termino," in which the forelegs swing outward from the knee during the stride. The paso gaits are smooth, balanced and elegant, with a rapid beat and dynamic energy.

THE TRANSITIONS

Transitions are changes from one gait to another, to or from a halt, or changes of speed and balance within a gait. In nature, horses make transitions easily and automatically. Under the rider, they become a test of the horse's suppleness and responsiveness and the rider's skill.

When free, horses usually make transitions gradually—that is, they move from a halt to a walk and then into a trot, a canter, etc. In riding, we often want the horse to make a transition from one gait to another without intermediate steps—from a walk to a canter or from a canter to a halt. This is more difficult and requires especially good balance and suppleness.

For a smooth and prompt transition, the rider must prepare his horse for the transi-

FIGURE **16** *Transitions*

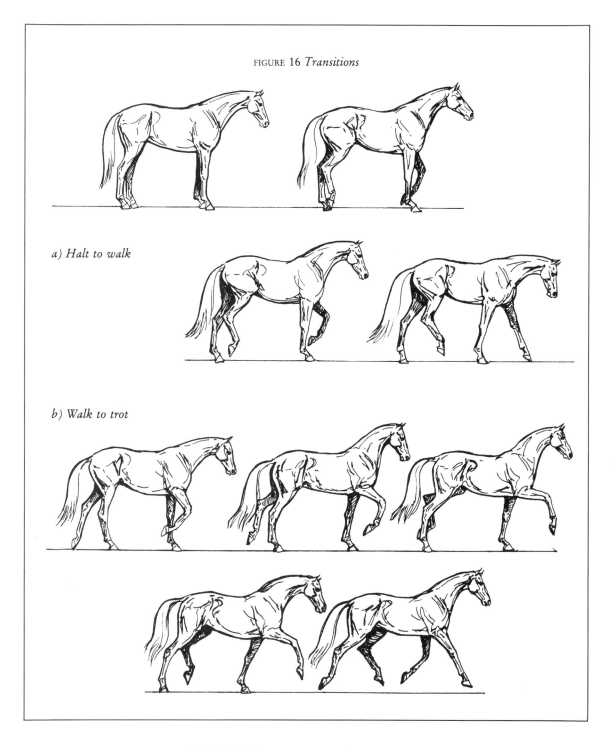

a) *Halt to walk*

b) *Walk to trot*

tion, apply the correct aids and time his aids perfectly. He must also remain in balance with the horse as the horse's gait changes; toppling forward or backward will upset the horse.

Timing of the aids is especially important. For example, a hind leg can only respond to the rider's leg aid to engage more when it is pushing off or swinging through the air—it cannot respond when it is on the ground bearing weight. In the canter, the horse can flex at the poll better and elevate his forehand more easily if the rider asks him to do so at the point in the canter when the forehand is coming up; if he asks when the forehand is reaching out and down, the horse cannot respond correctly at that instant.

By studying the sequence of the gaits and the transitions, we can learn when the aids can be best applied to get the transition smoothly and naturally. However, the rider will have to translate his intellectual knowledge into "feel" before he can put it into practice with good timing.

THE JUMP

The jump is a movement, not a gait. The jump can be executed from any gait or from a standstill, but it is most often performed from the canter.

There are five phases to the jump: the approach, takeoff, flight, landing and recovery.

FIGURE 17 *Transitions*

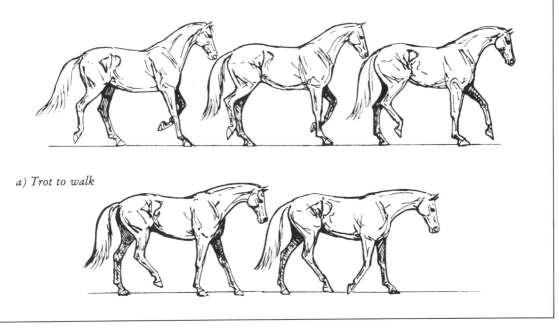

a) Trot to walk

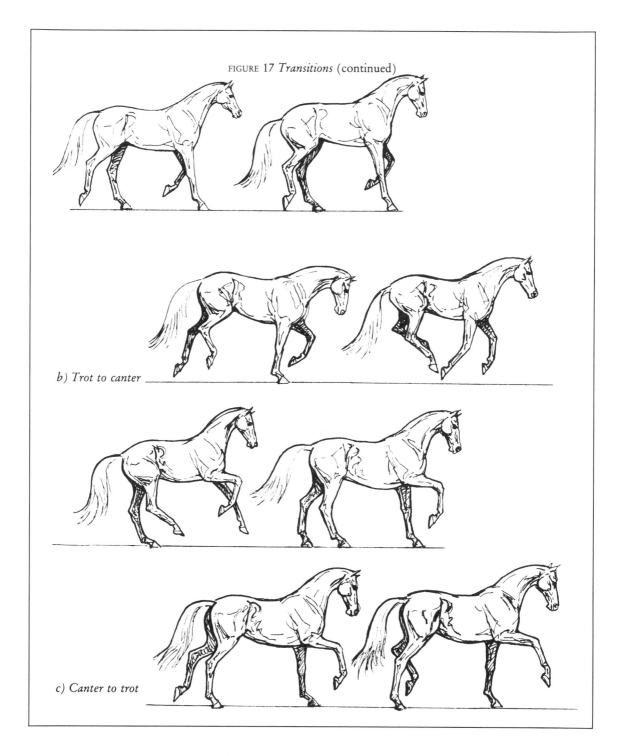

FIGURE 17 *Transitions* (continued)

b) Trot to canter

c) Canter to trot

HORSE GAITS, BALANCE AND MOVEMENT

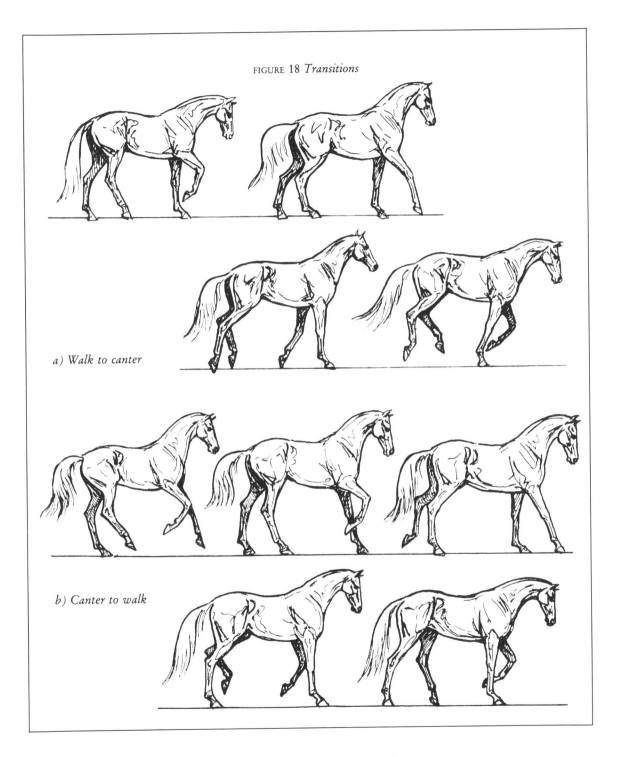

FIGURE 18 *Transitions*

a) Walk to canter

b) Canter to walk

THE GAITS AND TRANSITIONS

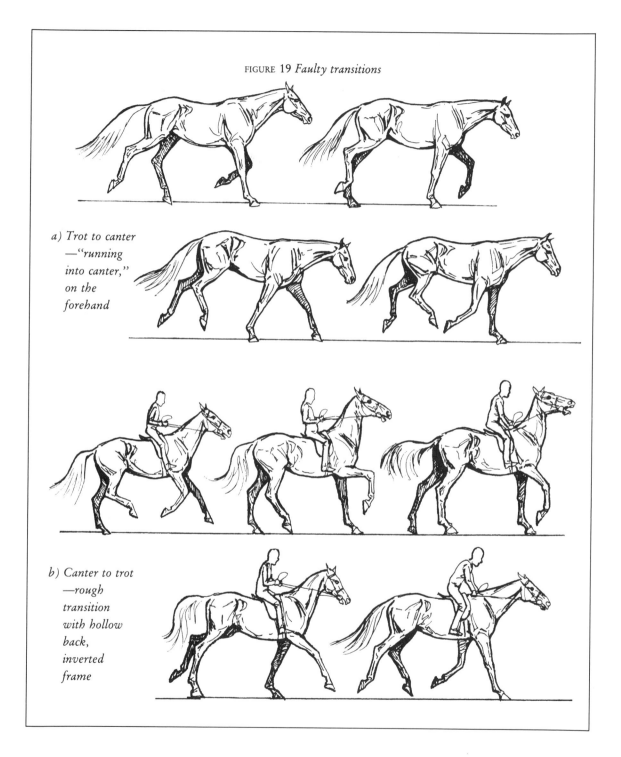

FIGURE **19** *Faulty transitions*

a) Trot to canter —"running into canter," on the forehand

b) Canter to trot —rough transition with hollow back, inverted frame

Ideally, the horse jumps most obstacles "in stride"—that is, the length of the jump is equal to the length of his canter stride and the jump is performed in rhythm. Some jumps require extraordinary effort and are not jumped in stride.

Phases of the Jump

APPROACH   During the approach, the horse sees the jump, judges the effort needed to clear it and adjusts his direction, balance, impulsion and stride to arrive at the right takeoff point from which to leave the ground. He needs a well-balanced, rhythmic canter that allows him to adjust his stride easily and permits maximum engagement of the hind legs. Because of the way he sees, he must raise or lower his head to focus his eyes on the jump, which makes freedom of head and neck essential. A straight line to the center of the jump, continuing on to his destination, establishes his direction.

An unbalanced, irregular gait or a weaving, ambiguous approach make it very difficult for the horse to arrive safely at a good takeoff point. Sudden last-minute adjustments of stride, balance or impulsion are hard for both horse and rider, and can leave the horse handicapped at takeoff or even unable to jump. A high, restricted head carriage can make it difficult for the horse to see the jump and judge its size and the best takeoff point.

TAKEOFF   The horse engages both hind legs well under the body, flexing his loin and lumbosacral joint. The hind legs should be lined up together for maximum thrust. The horse "sits" on his hindquarters as the forehand rises and the forelegs leave the ground, then extends both hind legs to thrust his body up and forward. The thrust of the takeoff determines the height and width of his jump— once airborne, he cannot lift himself higher. In the meantime, the forelegs are brought forward and up by rotating the shoulders, and folded to avoid hitting the obstacle.

The balance and thrust of the takeoff are critical. Failure to engage both hind legs, to push off strongly enough or "leaving off one hind leg" robs the horse of power and scope. If the horse is slow to raise his forehand or fold his forelegs, or if his shoulders do not rotate sufficiently, he may "hang" his knees and hit the fence in front. Hitting an obstacle with a foreleg, especially above the knees, is more likely to cause the horse to fall and hence is considered a most serious fault.

FLIGHT   The horse leaves the ground and rounds his spine in a bascule as he passes over the obstacle. His neck reaches forward and down, his back is rounded and the lumbosacral joint flexes, bringing his hind legs up and folding them to clear the jump. As the hind legs pass over the highest point of the jump, the horse extends his back, raises his neck and begins to unfold his forelegs and extend them for landing.

Jumping with a stiff, restricted back and a retracted neck prevents a good bascule and causes a stiff, inhibited jump. The forelegs cannot be lifted as high or folded as tightly as they should, and the hind legs may trail lower

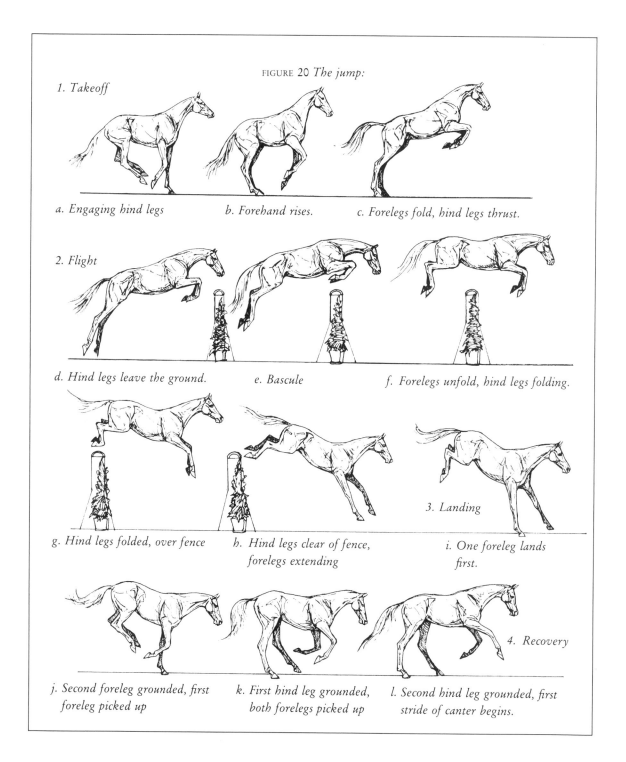

FIGURE 20 *The jump:*

1. Takeoff

a. Engaging hind legs   *b. Forehand rises.*   *c. Forelegs fold, hind legs thrust.*

2. Flight

d. Hind legs leave the ground.   *e. Bascule*   *f. Forelegs unfold, hind legs folding.*

3. Landing

g. Hind legs folded, over fence   *h. Hind legs clear of fence, forelegs extending*   *i. One foreleg lands first.*

4. Recovery

j. Second foreleg grounded, first foreleg picked up   *k. First hind leg grounded, both forelegs picked up*   *l. Second hind leg grounded, first stride of canter begins.*

and hit the obstacle. This is often caused by a rider falling behind the motion and interfering with the horse's use of his back, or restricting the horse's use of his neck with the reins. A desperate horse may perform "acrobatics"—he may snatch up his legs convulsively, twist sideways, make desperate swimming motions or extend his forelegs early; he may even try to put a foot down on top of the obstacle, usually with disastrous results!

LANDING   The horse lands on one extended foreleg first, quickly followed by the second foreleg. The body pivots forward over both forelegs, which are usually picked up before the first hind leg touches the ground. The second hind leg quickly follows. The first foreleg to land establishes the canter lead; since the forelegs and hind legs are evenly folded during the jump, it is easy for the horse to change leads over a jump or to select the lead he prefers to land on. The landing should be balanced, coordinated and elastic; the horse absorbs the first shock with the muscles of the shoulders, arm and forearm and the joints and tendons of the foreleg.

A stiff, unbalanced or rough landing is hard on both horse and rider and can injure the horse. Insufficient impulsion and balance can cause the horse to land heavily on his front legs—this makes it hard for him to resume his canter and on difficult ground can lead to a fall. Some horses land unevenly to spare a weak or sore leg; they may always land on a preferred lead. Rider interference, especially dropping down onto the horse's back, can cause the horse to drop his hind legs prematurely, landing more or less on all four legs at once. This is rough, painful and very hard on the horse's back.

RECOVERY   The horse recovers his normal balance and resumes the canter. The better balanced the jump, the more smoothly the horse can recover. The horse must regain his canter rhythm and balance as quickly as possible. When the horse jumps in stride and lands in good balance, his recovery is quick, natural and effortless and his first stride is ready to go on.

Landing unbalanced or with insufficient impulsion makes recovery an effort. A delayed recovery makes the horse slow in getting away from the fence and makes it harder to adjust his balance and stride for the next effort. Some horses become tense and quick, bucking or running away from the effort of recovery or the unpleasant experience of jumping. Deep, muddy ground can delay the horse in picking up his forelegs after landing; this can result in overreaching, an injury that occurs when a hind foot "grabs" the heel or tendon of the foreleg. If a horse makes a bad mistake and loses his balance when landing, he may "peck," throwing his head down and forward like a bird pecking at the ground in an effort to keep from going down.

5

GAIT QUALITIES
AND GOOD MOVEMENT

When we look at movement, we are looking at how the horse uses himself. Horses (and humans) can use their body mechanism well or poorly. Misuse of the horse's mechanism is inefficient, ugly and damaging; good movement is easy, beautiful and lets the horse reach his maximum potential. We need to be able to recognize good and poor use of the horse's body in order to ride, train or judge him and to keep him sound.

Good movement is functional. It is the best way for a horse to move in order to do his job. While there are many different types of movement that are related to specific horse breeds, types and disciplines, there are some qualities that apply to all movement. By looking at these qualities, we can judge whether any kind of movement is good or bad.

Good movement is natural and efficient. The horse's muscles and mechanism work harmoniously, without overstressing any part of the body. This allows the horse to perform longer with less fatigue and stress and helps him to stay sound. Horses that move well are less likely to injure themselves or break down than poor movers, and they often remain sound and useful well into old age.

Good movement, which is more comfortable for the rider and is easier to ride than poor movement, allows the horse to be in better balance and makes it easier for him to carry his rider in comfort. (Good riding certainly helps, too!)

Good movement allows maximum performance. When the horse uses his body mechanism in the best possible way, he can perform at the peak of his own ability. This means a bigger jump, more dynamic movement, greater speed, more ability to stop, turn or do whatever his special job requires.

Finally, good movement is beautiful. Even a plain-looking horse can be transformed when he moves really well.

GAIT QUALITIES

What makes good movement? There are a number of essential elements or gait qualities that go into good movement, no matter what the horse's job. These are just as important to a racing Standardbred as they are to a dressage horse, a jumper or a western pleasure horse.

Rhythm and Tempo

Every gait is performed in its own rhythm, which includes the beats and the pattern of footfalls in each stride. Good movement has a clear, consistent rhythm, without shuffling, mixing gaits or irregularities. Cadence is the clarity of the rhythm; for instance, marching has a clearer cadence than sauntering along at a walk. Tempo refers to the speed of the rhythm—quick, medium or slow. (Don't confuse tempo with speed or miles per hour of the gait, which depends on length of stride as well as tempo.) The tempo of the gait should stay the same even when the horse lengthens or shortens stride or performs various maneuvers. Each horse has his own best working tempo for each gait that lets him move his best.

Inconsistent and irregular gaits are difficult to ride and waste the horse's energy. Quickening or speeding up the tempo too much is called "running"—this produces a tense, irregular gait and makes it difficult for the horse to keep his balance; it goes with a tense or confused mental attitude. Lazy horses let the tempo slow down until they "break down" to a slower gait.

Impulsion

Impulsion is thrust. It comes from the horse's desire to go forward with energy, willingness and power, but without rushing. Impulsion gives the gaits liveliness and animation. In order to have impulsion the horse must be willing to go forward and must travel straight. (Crookedness inhibits thrust.)

Impulsion is *not* speed, nervousness or wild runaway energy. In order to have impulsion, the horse must engage his hind legs and allow the energy to come through his elastic back. "Going forward" means using the hind legs powerfully, not just going fast. A horse may have great impulsion at slow gaits, or even at a standstill (as in a piaffe or in a racehorse in the starting gate). A horse that is holding back, tiring or scrambling along with little engagement lacks impulsion, even if he is going fast.

Calmness and Relaxation

Calmness is mental relaxation. Horses need calmness in order to accept and understand the rider's aids and concentrate on their work. Horses that lack calmness are easily distracted, confused and physically tense. Lack of calmness can lead to hysteria, resistance and "blowing up" under stress.

All good athletes need a certain degree of physical relaxation in order to move with ease, grace and coordination. Every muscle goes through a cycle of contraction and relaxation with each stride. Tension and stiffness are the opposite of relaxation; they hamper athletic movement and cause discomfort, awkwardness, mistakes and even injuries.

FIGURE 1 *Impulsion vs. speed*

a) Horse tiring or holding back lacks impulsion, even at a fast gait.

b) Great impulsion is shown in the piaffe, a trot in place.

laxation can degenerate into laziness. The optimum combination of calmness, relaxation and impulsion is usually found when the horse is in his best working rhythm and tempo.

Horses give several *signs of relaxation* that the rider should recognize, especially when working with a horse that is inclined to be tense. These signs say, "I'm okay," or "Now I can move well," or "I understand." Three signs to watch for are a deep breath (like a sigh), gently chewing (like swallowing), and blowing the nose in a long, relaxed snort. When the horse gives one or more of these relaxation signs, his movement often improves. In training, it is a good idea to acknowledge such signs from the horse with a pat or a word of approval.

Balance

The horse must work in the best balance for the task he has to perform. Horses do this

Calmness and relaxation balance out energy. Without relaxation, the forward urge could make the horse tense up until he became uncontrollable; without impulsion, re-

naturally when they are free, but the problem of carrying a rider affects any horse's balance. Some learn better than others to handle this balance problem, but many horses fall into a habit of moving in poor balance because they have never learned any other way to cope with carrying a rider. Some horses are naturally better balanced, better coordinated and more athletic than others, ridden or free—just as some people are gifted athletes and others are less so. The skill of the rider makes a big difference—it is much easier for a horse to move in good balance under a rider who has control of his own balance, and an unbalanced or awkward rider can handicap the most athletic horse.

A moving horse's balance is dynamic, not static—that is, it is fluid and makes constant small and large changes. However, for every gait, movement and circumstance there is an optimum "average" balance that allows the horse to move at his best. A supple, well-balanced horse has control of his balance and can shift it quickly to cope with changes of speed, direction, terrain or the requests of his rider. A horse that is "stuck" in a certain mode of balance (for example, one that moves with too much weight on the forehand) has fewer options and less freedom to shift his balance and move well.

Poor balance can interfere with movement and control in all kinds of ways. Loss of balance is scary and distracting for both horse and rider. Even if the horse is trying to obey his rider's wishes, he may be incapable of responding promptly if he is preoccupied with struggling with his balance. If a horse

moves with too much weight on the forehand at fast gaits (and perhaps his rider's weight is too far forward, too), he may feel that he has to quicken his tempo until he is scrambling to keep up with his balance, the way a child running downhill must run faster and faster so as not to fall down. Many runaways are really only "balance runaways" and are not exhibiting willful disobedience; poor balance distresses the horse as much as it does the rider.

Straightness

Good movement is straight, not swinging inward or outward, and not canted off to one side or cranked sideways. This is more efficient and allows impulsion to come through unhampered, and does not run the risk of the horse damaging his legs by interfering (striking one leg against the other) or overstressing one side of his feet and legs. Straightness allows the rider to ride more accurately; the horse may use crookedness to evade the rider's control. Like humans, all horses have a stronger side and a weaker side. Consequently, they tend to be naturally crooked to some degree, and true straightness must be developed through training.

There are two kinds of straightness in movement. The first refers to the flight of each leg and the way the foot lands. Horses with good leg conformation move each leg relatively straight, without swinging inward or outward. This is sometimes called moving true. Crooked leg conformation causes deviations in movement. Swinging inward (wing-

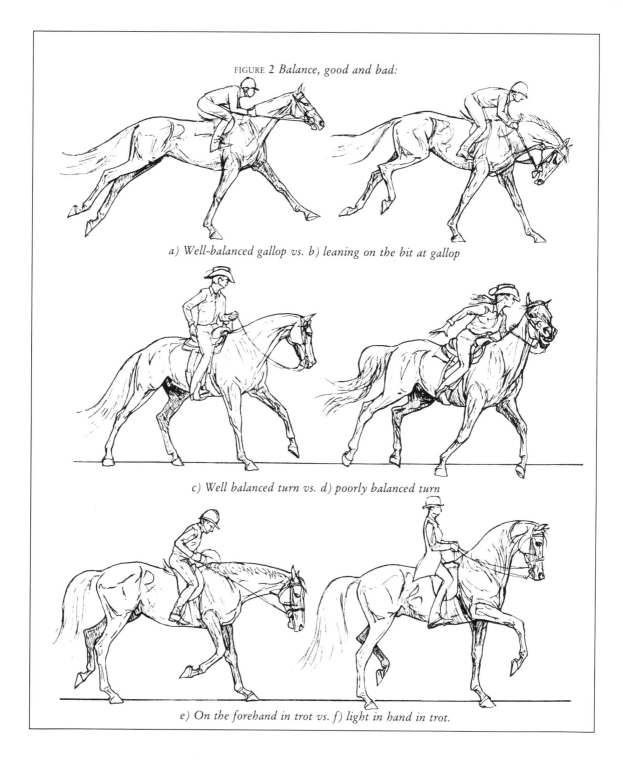

FIGURE 2 *Balance, good and bad:*

a) Well-balanced gallop vs. b) leaning on the bit at gallop

c) Well balanced turn vs. d) poorly balanced turn

e) On the forehand in trot vs. f) light in hand in trot.

FIGURE 3 *A "balance runaway"*

ing in) is apt to cause interference (the horse strikes one foot against the opposite leg). This is associated with toed-out conformation. Swinging outward (paddling) does not lead to interference injuries but can cause the foot to land unevenly, putting more stress on one side of the foot and leg; this results from toed-in conformation. Horses with base-narrow conformation sometimes place one foot in front of another (plaiting, or rope-walking), which can be dangerous as well as inefficient; it can cause a stumble. These kinds of crooked movement can be helped to some extent by corrective shoeing.

The other meaning of straightness refers to the movement of the whole horse and his spinal alignment. His hind legs should follow in the tracks of his front legs, which is called tracking straight. This means that he will be straight when moving on a straight line, and will bend laterally on turns and curves. This helps to keep this spinal column aligned properly and permits freer, more efficient and more graceful movement than crookedness. A horse that turns with his body stiff like a board in the water, or that bends his body and neck to the outside of a turn feels awkward and uncoordinated. A horse that moves slightly sideways with his hindquarters or shoulders crooked cannot move with maximum freedom, impulsion and efficiency; one side of his body is stiffer than the other.

All horses have one side they prefer, just as most people are right- or left-handed. Some horsemen believe this may be related to the way the foal is carried in his dam, or to the fact that most horses are handled more from the left than the right. Riders sometimes make this situation worse by riding crookedly

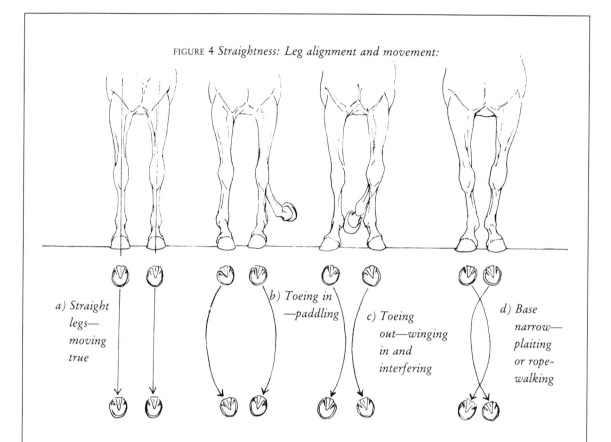

FIGURE 4 *Straightness: Leg alignment and movement:*

a) Straight legs—moving true

b) Toeing in —paddling

c) Toeing out—winging in and interfering

d) Base narrow— plaiting or rope-walking

themselves, or by allowing the horse to work only in his preferred direction until he becomes one-sided—weak on one side and overdeveloped on the other. Weakness, injury or unsoundness can cause a horse to favor one side and overdevelop the other to compensate. A one-sided horse finds it difficult to pick up one lead and will be awkward in turning toward his stiff side. He will not want to accept contact with the bit on his hollow side, but may lean on the bit on the stiff side. One goal of training is to develop the horse's sides as evenly as possible and to make the horse more nearly straight. The less difference between the two sides, the straighter the horse can move and the easier it is to achieve pure, classical movement in any gait.

Suppleness

Suppleness is the ability of the horse to shift his balance smoothly forward and backward as well as laterally (sideways) without stiff-

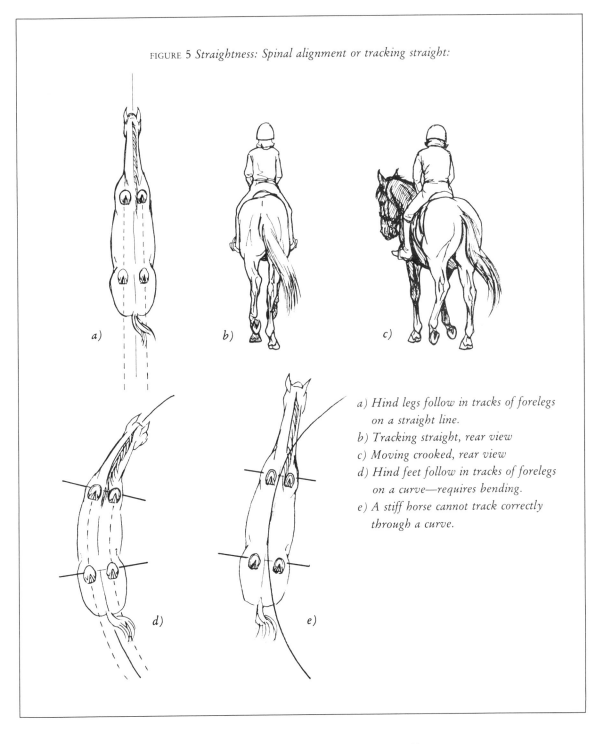

FIGURE 5 *Straightness: Spinal alignment or tracking straight:*

a)

b)

c)

d)

e)

a) *Hind legs follow in tracks of forelegs on a straight line.*
b) *Tracking straight, rear view*
c) *Moving crooked, rear view*
d) *Hind feet follow in tracks of forelegs on a curve—requires bending.*
e) *A stiff horse cannot track correctly through a curve.*

GAIT QUALITIES AND GOOD MOVEMENT

ness or resistance. It is related to balance and straightness. A supple horse can easily respond to his rider's requests to lengthen, shorten, change gaits, change movements, turn or shift his balance. This shows especially in smooth, prompt and fluid transitions.

Stiffness is the opposite of suppleness. A stiff horse is awkward, clumsy and slow to respond to his rider, even if he is willing. A supple horse is flexible, limber and adaptable. However, don't confuse suppleness with excessive neck flexibility, which is called rubbernecking. This happens when the horse lacks impulsion and weaves, twists and sidles instead of moving honestly forward. Such action, which makes the horse very difficult to control, is often caused by misguided training methods that attempt to "supple" a horse by forcibly overbending his neck from side to side without attending to other gait qualities like impulsion and balance.

Freedom of Movement

Freedom of movement means the extent to which the horse can reach forward in movement from his hip joints and shoulders. Freedom of movement allows big, athletic gaits and fluid movement with scope and amplitude; its opposite would be short, constrained and restricted gaits. While a gifted mover with outstanding conformation has an advantage when it comes to freedom of movement, this depends on how the horse uses what nature gave him. Freedom of movement comes from lively impulsion and

FIGURE 6 *Rubbernecking—bending neck near withers*

suppleness of the joints and muscles, free from the paralyzing effects of resistance. A rather ordinary-looking horse may use himself superbly and "dance" through his movements with great verve and freedom, while a horse with more perfect conformation may be musclebound, stiff and resistant or unwilling to use himself freely.

Lightness

Lightness is the horse's ability to move with deftness, agility and grace. It is the result of

FIGURE 7

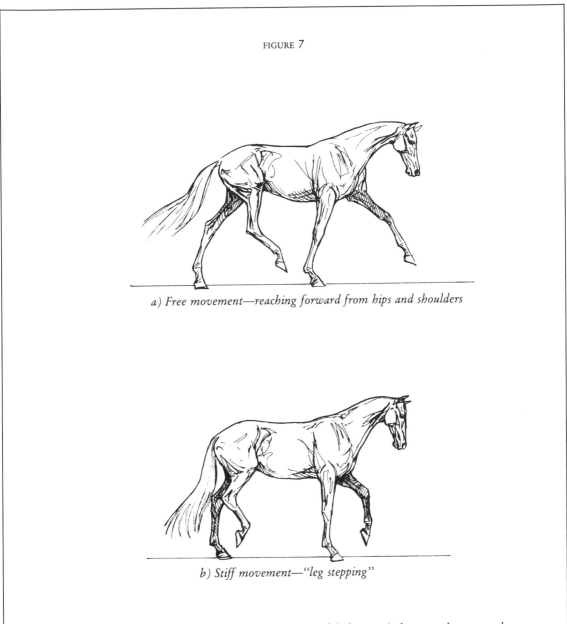

a) Free movement—reaching forward from hips and shoulders

b) Stiff movement—"leg stepping"

suppleness, impulsion, balance and freedom of movement. A horse that is light to ride is handy, balanced and responsive. The opposite of lightness is heavy, clumsy and uncoordinated movement.

6

BALANCE AND MOVEMENT

The horse knows how to use his balance from an hour or so after birth. Once a foal has learned to stand up and coordinate his legs, he can trot, gallop, leap and buck—most of the time, he doesn't give balance a single thought. On the rare occasions that he miscalculates and loses his balance or slips—perhaps he takes a corner too fast while chasing another colt, or encounters ice or slippery ground—he receives an instantaneous lesson on what works and what doesn't. Human babies learn to toddle, climb and run the same way, except that it takes us much longer.

As he starts being ridden, the horse experiences balance problems he never had before. He must learn to use his body to carry and balance the weight of the rider. This makes green colts awkward and ungainly until they become accustomed to carrying weight and become strong enough to handle it without strain. Coping with the problem of balancing the rider is easier if the rider is skillful and supple and can ride in balance with the horse. A stiff, insecure and unbalanced rider is very hard to carry. The greatest difficulty, though, is that the horse must move when, how and where the rider tells him—and he may have trouble understanding what the rider is trying to tell him. Any simple movement such as walking becomes a problem if you must do it precisely according to someone else's directions and timing, although you could do it easily and naturally if allowed to do it your own way. How much harder would it be to do this while carrying a small alien being from outer space on your shoulders, who directs your movements in a language that you do not completely understand and who may get in your way but can punish you if you do it wrong? The tension created by your awkward balance and inability to understand makes it even harder to move in balance, creating a vicious circle.

Fortunately, most horses and riders get through the "alien" stage and achieve a more or less workable balance together. Any kind of movement, no matter how simple, is easier, safer and more efficient when performed with horse and rider in good balance together. Any loss of balance, no matter how slight, is uncomfortable, scary and inhibits good movement. Because poor balance feels bad to both horse and rider, some problems can be solved naturally by trial and error if the rider is sensitive to the horse's difficulties. However, this works best in uncomplicated natural activities that do not require a high degree of balance, and in which the horse can see what he has to do, like easy trail riding. When the job becomes critical and demands a high degree of balance, as in working at speed, jumping sizable fences or performing advanced movements, the rider must be educated enough to help the horse with his balance and must be very supple and well balanced himself.

Misunderstanding of movement and balance leads some riders and trainers to force their horses into ways of moving that defeat their purposes. Trying to create a certain mode of balance by forcing the head to do this, the hocks to do that, while the shoulders do something else, misses the point: good movement comes from good balance along with other essential gait qualities, not from putting the pieces together. Using anxiety techniques or fear to make the horse gather itself into balance is even worse—the horse cannot move fluidly, although he may move athletically out of sheer desperation.

Such abusive training eventually results in physical or mental breakdown.

THE BASICS OF BALANCE

Center of Gravity

Understanding the horse's balance begins with his basic structure. His forehand is heavier than his hindquarters; a standing horse carries about 55 to 60 percent of his weight on his front legs and around 40 to 45 percent on the hind legs. The center of gravity is an imaginary spot at which his balance is said to be concentrated—his balance point. At a standstill, it is located near the heart girth, a little forward of the midpoint of the horse's body. The exact position of the center of gravity varies, depending on the individual horse's conformation and stance. Raising the head shifts the center of gravity

FIGURE 1 *Location of horse's center of gravity when standing still*

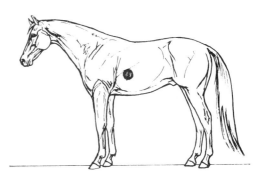

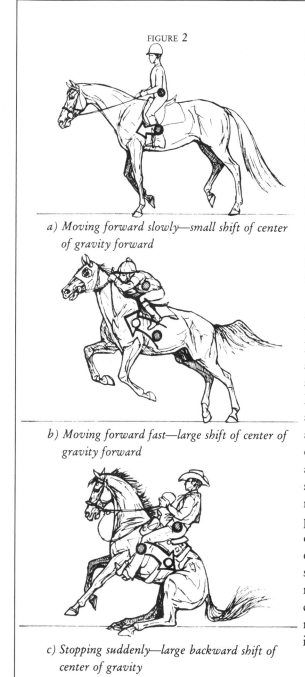

FIGURE 2

a) Moving forward slowly—small shift of center of gravity forward

b) Moving forward fast—large shift of center of gravity forward

c) Stopping suddenly—large backward shift of center of gravity

backward a little; lowering the head shifts it forward. The horse's legs must support the center of gravity or he would fall down.

When the horse moves forward, his center of gravity shifts forward. His legs must reach forward in time to catch his balance or he will fall down on his nose. If he moves forward slowly, without leaning forward much, the center of gravity shifts forward only a tiny bit and requires only a small stride. If his forward movement is big and violent, like a racehorse breaking from a standing start, his center of gravity also shifts suddenly and extremely forward and requires a bigger reach forward to catch it.

Once in motion, the center of gravity is never quite still but makes small or large fluctuations with each phase of the stride. The horse's balance in motion is dynamic, not static. However, his center of gravity can be said to be in an *average* position—more or less forward, according to the speed and balance of the gait. A collected gait, performed at a steady speed on level ground without changing direction, has the most stable balance but is never completely static. At a long-striding gallop, the center of gravity oscillates more because there are greater changes in the position of the head, neck, back and hindquarters at each phase of the stride. However, even a racing gallop can be relatively stable in balance if the horse keeps a steady rhythm and speed and makes no major changes. Changes of direction, speed and terrain cause greater shifts in the center of gravity as the horse moves.

When stopping or slowing down, the center of gravity shifts backward. The horse's technique when stopping can make a difference—if he engages his hind legs and "sits" on his haunches, the center of gravity shifts smoothly backward and down, but if he throws his weight forward and brakes to a stiff-legged stop with his forelegs, the center of gravity "bounces" backward, forward and upward until the horse comes to a stop. This is unhandy and uncomfortable for both horse and rider.

Lateral Balance

The horse's lateral (side-to-side) balance is more difficult to handle than his longitudinal (front-to-back) balance. His center of gravity is in his heavy body, suspended fairly high over a narrow base of support. His best way of coping with lateral balance is to engage his hind legs, shifting his balance backward and freeing his forehand to reach out sideways as necessary to maintain his center of gravity. The horse's ability to rotate his spine and reach sideways with his legs helps him be agile and handy in turning and moving sideways. Horses that are built compact and low to the ground are often better at lateral balance and agility than large, long-legged and rangy horses.

In turning, the hind leg on the inside of the turn is a major key to balance. The better engaged the inside hind leg, the easier it is for the horse to control his balance in a turn. If his inside hind leg is not where it should be or if it slips, he is much more apt to slip or fall.

FIGURE 3 *Balance in turns:*

a) Inside hind leg engaged in a bending turn

b) Inside hind leg engaged in a turn at speed

c) Abrupt turn at speed—off balance, failing to engage inside hind leg

A horse whose balance is too much on the forehand is much more likely to slip when turning sharply or on slippery ground, and has less chance to recover his balance, mostly because his inside hind leg is not as well engaged. Horses that experience difficulty with lateral balance often slow down or break down to a slower gait in order to recover. They are also prone to get scared and scramble, increasing their speed. This is especially common in green horses when learning to canter on a circle.

Modes of Balance

Like humans, horses can move in different postures or modes of balance—leaning backward or leaning forward, so to speak. We humans do the same thing when we lean forward while hiking up a steep hill or pushing a wheelbarrow, or shift our weight back when going downstairs. When an athlete (horse or human) needs to be ready for action, he "gathers himself," and he may slouch along in a relaxed posture when he is tired or idle.

Modes of balance include:

COLLECTION   The horse gathers himself for action by engaging his hindquarters, shifting his balance backward and lightening his forehand. His back rounds in a bascule and his neck arches and rises, especially at the base. His head is carried high and he flexes at the poll, which is the highest point of the horse. His movement becomes light and mobile, with shorter, higher strides and active hindquarters, and he is able to shift his balance

instantly in any direction. Collection implies that the horse's mechanism is "cocked"; he has great impulsion at his command and can move dynamically. Collection also implies heightened attention and awareness; in nature, it is seen in moments of excitement.

WORKING GAITS   The horse is somewhat collected; he engages his hindquarters and adopts a balance in which he can best carry the rider and move in his best working rhythm. Working gaits are shown by horses that are not yet trained or ready for fully collected gaits. They lie between collected and medium gaits.

MEDIUM GAITS   These lie between collected and extended gaits. The horse moves with good balance and somewhat extended strides in a "round" outline, with an elastic back, a rounded back and a somewhat arched neck. The movement shows lightness, rhythm and elevation as well as length of stride, with lively impulsion from the hindquarters.

EXTENDED GAITS   The horse moves with great impulsion from the hindquarters and extends his stride to the utmost, covering the most possible ground with each stride. The hind legs are well engaged, the back is round and elastic and the neck is arched but lengthened, with nose pointing somewhat forward. The horse does not lean forward against the bit but remains in balance. His gait remains regular, rhythmic and in the same tempo, without running or quickening. The balance is somewhat more backward than many peo-

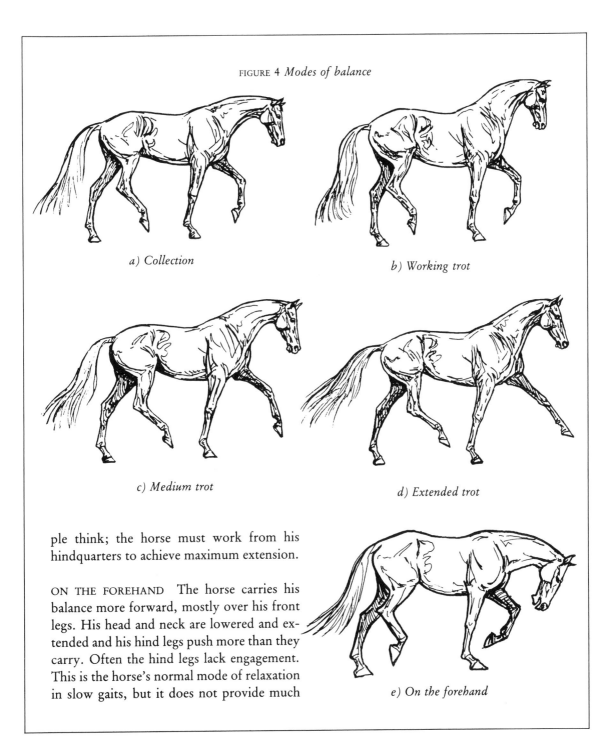

FIGURE 4 *Modes of balance*

a) Collection

b) Working trot

c) Medium trot

d) Extended trot

ple think; the horse must work from his hindquarters to achieve maximum extension.

ON THE FOREHAND The horse carries his balance more forward, mostly over his front legs. His head and neck are lowered and extended and his hind legs push more than they carry. Often the hind legs lack engagement. This is the horse's normal mode of relaxation in slow gaits, but it does not provide much

e) On the forehand

impulsion or ability to shift the balance promptly. Sometimes a horse may move too much on the forehand in a fast "running" gait.

Balance Problems

Horses often have less than perfect balance when being ridden, partly because of the difficulties of carrying their riders and obeying the rider's wishes, and partly because of their own imperfect balance and movement. Balance problems are usually easier to solve in relatively slow, stable working gaits like the trot than at speed. Some activities, like jumping or reining, and some conditions, like slippery ground or working uphill and downhill, demand a higher degree of balance and suppleness from the horse.

Balance problems usually stem from being too much on the forehand and failure to engage the hind legs enough for the movement. Stiffness, fatigue, inexperience, rider problems and some conformation problems make

it harder for the horse to learn to handle his balance.

Calm horses often cope with a minor loss of balance by slowing down or breaking gait, just as a running person tries to slow down if he starts to lose his balance. However, fear and tension caused by losing their balance, along with the instinct to flee from any scary situation, make many horses scramble and speed up when their balance is threatened. This may be poor judgment, but it is the horse's natural instinct. It can lead to a damaging cycle of fear, tension, speed and worse and worse balance until either the horse is in real trouble or the rider intervenes.

THE HORSE'S FRAME

The horse's outline and posture are sometimes referred to as a frame. A horse may be said to be working in a short frame when he is collected and in a long frame when his back, neck and strides are long and low. The

FIGURE 5

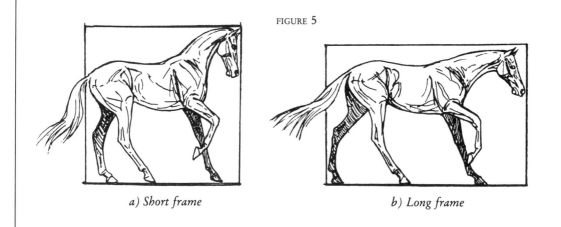

a) Short frame   *b) Long frame*

frame includes the carriage and posture of the head and neck, the back and the engagement and length of stride of the hind legs. It is sometimes used to describe a typical outline and posture expected in a certain level or type of event, such as a "training-level dressage frame," a "fourth-level dressage frame," or a "western pleasure frame."

Unfortunately, the idea of "putting the horse in a frame" is open to misunderstanding and abuse. Some trainers have an "ideal" frame that they would like the horse to move in; this ideal may be based on the silhouette of a champion or the ideal horse of their type. However, the exact outline in which a horse moves his best is a very individual thing, and too much emphasis on the frame at the expense of the movement is like trying to force a square peg into a round hole. If the horse is

made to carry his head and neck in a certain posture, and his hocks are then driven forward until the outline appears right, the horse may achieve a frame that "looks right" according to the trainer's ideas, but that is difficult, constrained, and unnatural for him. This stiffens the horse and paralyzes his movement, and can set up resistances that can be very difficult to eradicate. It can even damage the horse physically.

The term "frame" is harmless when used descriptively: "That horse should work in a shorter frame," or "That's a nice frame for a hunter." As a training goal, it can easily be misused. It is more important to produce the best movement your horse is capable of than to try to put him into a predetermined frame or outline, which may ultimately hamper his movement.

7

POOR MOVEMENT

There are several syndromes of faulty movement that may show up in any type of horse. All make a horse difficult to ride and prevent him from reaching his full potential; each can eventually damage the horse. In all of the following syndromes, the horse's natural movement is distorted and his circle of muscles is not used in a balanced and coordinated way; the horse fails to engage his hind legs well under his body. Poor movement may be the result of conformation defects, unsoundness, uncoordination or weakness, but it is most often caused by bad riding and training. Because these kinds of faulty movement are difficult to ride, unathletic and damaging to the horse, besides being unattractive, they should be heavily penalized when judging horse movement and the results of training.

INVERTED FRAME (ABOVE THE BIT)

The horse moves with a stiff, hollow back, high head and tense neck, and short strides that lack engagement. The head is carried above the normal angle of control with a stiff poll and jaw and with the nose poked out ("stargazing"). The horse is usually tense, nervous and fretful, and may prance, toss his head and pull against the bit. The circle of muscles is disengaged and the back is locked and stiffened, especially at the lumbosacral joint, which makes the gaits rough and almost impossible to sit. The strides are irregular, often with a too-fast "running" tempo.

This syndrome is often seen in hot, tense horses that are forcibly restrained. It is one of the most damaging to the horse and most difficult to ride. The stiff back and neck cause back soreness and eventually lead to damage to the back and legs, especially the hocks. The horse may develop an "under neck"—bulging muscles on the underside of the neck from stiffening his neck against the bit. The high head carriage makes it difficult for the horse to see where he is going, and a bad head-tosser may hit the rider in the face with his head. Because of the difficulty of sitting correctly on an inverted horse, the rider often sits out of balance, with his legs ahead. This is hard on the horse's back and can create a situation in which the horse becomes even more severely inverted and the rider sits worse and worse in his efforts to cope.

To correct the inverted horse, he must first be slowed down and calmed down. The rider must ride in good balance, treating the horse's back softly and allowing the back and neck muscles to relax and stretch; he should post, not sit to the trot. He must increase the horse's engagement and length of stride, particularly with the hind legs, in order to restore the circle of muscles to normal function. This takes tactful use of the leg aids and maintaining a good working rhythm and tempo. Forcing the head down with martingales and control devices will not solve the problem; the horse must learn to accept the bit with a relaxed mouth and poll and learn to reach out and down to the bit.

FALSE COLLECTION (BEHIND THE BIT)

The horse moves with a hollow back and lacks engagement as above, but his neck is arched and his head is carried at or behind the vertical. Instead of flexing at the poll, the flexion takes place farther back in the neck, causing a "broken neck" in which the poll is not the highest point of the neck. The horse may champ nervously or rigidly set his jaw, but he does not accept the bit or reach out to it, and he evades contact with the rider's hands. Because of his short, irregular strides and lack of engagement, his circle of muscles is ineffective. He moves in false collection, snapping his front legs up but failing to engage his hindquarters or use his back to lighten the forehand. His front and hind legs may lose coordination, and he may add extra beats to the stride in the trot and canter. The horse's ability to shift his balance is severely handicapped.

This syndrome is often seen when the horse is forced into a slow or falsely collected gait without using his hindquarters and back correctly. It often results when a trainer tries to correct an inverted horse by forcing his head and neck into a lower and more flexed position, especially through the use of severe bits or control devices like draw reins. If the horse does not engage his hind legs and improve the use of his back, he runs the same risk of damaging his mechanism as if he were moving inverted. He fakes collection by rounding his neck, but does not accept the bit or use his circle of muscles. He may evade the rider's control by overbending or by dropping his chin against his chest and using the strength of his neck to resist the rider. The overbent horse holds back instead of moving freely forward—in extreme cases, he may balk, whirl, back up or rear.

This syndrome is more difficult to cure than the inverted horse, but the principles are the same. The horse must engage his hind legs with long, regular strides and allow his back and neck to relax and lengthen. He must learn to accept the bit and the rider's seat and legs and reach out willingly to the bit in response to the rider's aids. The rider must ride in balance and free the horse's back to round up; he needs effective leg aids and especially tactful and educated hands to restore the horse's confidence in the bit and reestablish the use of his circle of muscles. He must be especially aware of the horse's use of his back and hind legs in rhythm, and must not be taken in by a fake head carriage.

ON THE FOREHAND

The horse moves with lazy, disengaged steps, with the hind legs pushing the weight onto the forehand instead of carrying their share. He travels with his head low and most of his weight on the front legs; his circle of muscles is slack and disengaged. He may hang heavily on the bit, and his movements are slow and clumsy. At faster gaits, he is prone to lose his balance forward and "run," and he may be hard to stop; when stopping, he tends to "brake" with his forelegs. He cannot make quick turns, movement or shifts of weight easily, and he may break down to a slower gait if asked to turn.

This is a normal attitude for tired or lazy horses and is often seen in young horses who are not yet used to carrying a rider. At slow gaits, it is an attitude of calmness and relaxation and is acceptable for resting and cooling out, as long as the horse does not become so sloppy that he is in danger of stumbling. When a horse moves habitually on the forehand, he is unhandy to ride and heavy in hand. He also overstresses his forelegs, which can in time lead to front leg problems. His ring of muscles becomes slack and underdeveloped, resulting in a hanging belly and an undermuscled top line. Horses often learn to go on the forehand when they are made to travel slowly without engaging their hind legs and shifting their balance backward.

To correct the horse that moves too much on the forehand, the rider must awaken the horse's impulsion and get him to engage his hind legs with longer, regular strides. The rider must sit in balance (riders often contribute to this problem by leaning too far forward) and must use effective, well-timed leg aids. Only when the horse is engaging his hind legs can the rider begin to use his hands to ask the horse to improve his head carriage—if he tries to correct the head position without engaging the hind legs, he will only make the problem worse.

FALSE EXTENSION, RETRACTED NECK

The horse moves energetically, but with a hollow, disengaged back and a stiff, shortened neck that retracts from the bit. The hind legs move with push-back engagement—they swing backward more than they reach forward. The forelegs are thrust forward with an exaggerated goose-stepping action that flips the toes up; because the forelegs are artificially extended, they must be retracted slightly before they strike the ground. The circle of muscles is disengaged and the front and hind legs are not quite coordinated; the horse loses the clarity of his rhythm and may add an extra beat to the trot or canter. In the walk, he may begin to pace.

This syndrome is usually the result of forcible and incorrect training and/or riding, particularly when the horse is driven hard against a rigid hand. It is often seen when the trainer demands a higher, more advanced head carriage without developing the horse's ability to engage his hind legs and use his back sufficiently. Forcing the head in while driving the horse forward may result in a vertical face and flexion at the poll, but the horse is cramped, constrained and artificial in his movements. Because of the exaggerated extension of the forelegs, the gait may appear spectacular to casual observers, but it is a travesty of the horse's true movement. The stiffness and extra effort of movement, combined with poor use of the back, neck, legs and circle of muscles, make this one of the most damaging forms of incorrect move-

ment. It often causes breakdowns in the hocks, the stifles or the back.

To restore correct movement, the horse must be allowed to find his natural carriage and rhythm in a longer, less constrained frame. The rider must be free and balanced in his own body in order to permit the horse to swing his back and regain his coordination. The horse must learn to reach out to the bit with his whole back and neck instead of retracting from it, and he must find the balance in which he can move with pure, coordinated gaits. The rider will have to approach collected and extended work very carefully, not asking the horse for more than he can do without constraint. Reclaiming a horse whose movement has been ruined in this manner requires a very good rider with a clear understanding of his goals and a great deal of sensitivity.

CROOKEDNESS

The horse does not move straight; his hind feet do not follow in the tracks of his front feet. He may carry his head, neck or hip to one side, tilt his head or move with his entire body canted sideways. He will have difficulty turning to one side and will prefer one lead at the canter; some crooked horses cannot canter at all on one lead. His contact with the bit is uneven—stronger on one side than the other. One hind leg does not engage as much as the other. The horse will be stiff and unhandy to ride, especially in turns, and will have trouble bending; he may travel bent to

FIGURE 1 *Incorrect and damaging forms of movement*

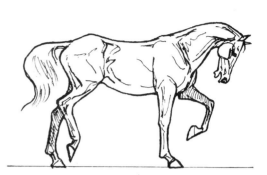

a) *Inverted frame—stiff, hollow back; above the bit; poor engagement*

b) *Behind the bit—hollow back; poor engagement; "broken neck" with incorrect flexion behind the poll*

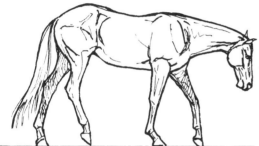

c) *On the forehand—poor engagement; leaning heavily on shoulders and forelegs*

d) *False extension—stiff, hollow back and retracted neck; incorrect "push-back" engagement; toe flipping*

the outside. Some horses "rubberneck" when asked to turn—they bend their necks sideways, but their body continues to go straight.

All horses have a side they prefer. One side is the hollow side (the side the horse prefers to bend toward); the other is the stiff side (the side on which he resists bending). A one-sided horse is weaker on one side and over-developed on the other. This may be due to unsoundness on one side, to habit (from always working in the same direction), or to a crooked rider. Many forms of crookedness are an effort to protect a weak or painful hind leg. Crooked horses try to avoid taking con-

FIGURE *2 Crookedness*

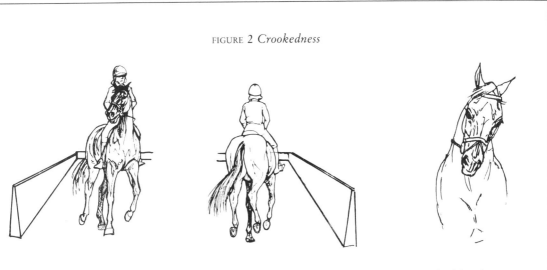

a) *"Popping a shoulder"—bent to the outside, misaligned spine*

b) *Crooked canter—hind legs carried to inside, misaligned spine*

c) *Tilted head—incorrect lateral flexion of poll*

tact with the bit on the hollow side of the mouth, but may lean or pull on the stiff side. Rubbernecked horses may have been pulled from side to side in a misguided effort to supple them; they do not connect rein aids with the body or the hind legs.

The crooked horse needs to stretch and strengthen both sides equally. He must develop suppleness (the ability to shift his balance easily) and lateral flexibility while moving forward. Working on circles, serpentines, broken lines and other schooling figures can help to improve bending and flexibility on his stiffer side. Lateral work, especially the shoulder-in, can help teach him to coordinate his body and move evenly and straight in both directions. The rider must be balanced (many riders are crooked or one-sided and don't realize it) and must under-

stand straightness and bending in order to help the horse. Tact is needed to teach the horse to soften on his stiff side and to accept a consistent contact on his hollow side. The rider must use his balance, his own body position and his leg aids and must avoid overuse of the hands and reins in straightening the horse. Since crookedness is often related to unsoundness, the first step should be a veterinary examination—you cannot train away a spavin!

IRREGULAR RHYTHM AND TEMPO

The horse moves with an uneven or inconsistent rhythm and tempo. He may speed up, quickening his tempo until he is "running" in his gait with a too-fast, uncontrolled rhythm, or he may move with a lazy, dragging tempo that threatens to break down to a slower gait at every step. An inconsistent horse speeds up and then slows down, constantly changing his tempo, speed and balance without warning. This is difficult to ride and is unsettling for the horse, too. The horse cannot move with relaxation and coordination if he is out of rhythm.

Rhythm and tempo problems often stem from the horse's mental attitude. If he is tense, upset, distracted or tuned out, it affects his rhythm, tempo and balance. "Running" gaits may occur when a horse is too much on the forehand and must move faster and faster for his legs to keep up with his balance; they can also happen when the horse is tense, confused or upset. (Some riders drive the horse into running gaits in an effort to obtain what they think is forward movement.) "Dragging" means moving with inadequate impulsion and engagement, usually with the horse too much on the forehand. Green horses are inconsistent; they react to the difficulties of turning, handling terrain or distractions by changing their speed, tempo and balance. Any horse, green or trained, may be inconsistent if his rider is not going with the movement in balance and rhythm with the horse, or if the aids are applied at random.

A rider with a good sense of rhythm can help the horse find a consistent tempo, rhythm, speed and balance. He can count, hum or sing under his breath to emphasize the rhythm and must apply his aids in rhythm with the horse's gait. At the trot he can adjust the speed of his posting to influence the horse's tempo, and he can use half-halts in rhythm at any gait to increase his horse's attention and balance. Above all, he must learn to recognize his horse's best working rhythm, balance and tempo and help the horse to keep it.

FORGING

Forging is a gait problem that occurs mostly at the trot and occasionally at the walk. If the foreleg is slow in breaking over and leaving the ground, the hind foot may forge, or click, striking the heel of the front shoe with the toe of the hind shoe. Forging indicates that the horse is moving too much on the forehand, which delays the foreleg in breaking over. Tired horses, green horses or immature colts are likely to forge. So are horses that are built with a very short back and long legs. A horse may forge because he is overdue for re-shoeing, or if he is shod with too long a toe and too low a heel, which delays breakover. Horses often forge when they reach the limits of their trotting stride and begin to "run" in the trot.

To eliminate forging, the horse's feet and shoes should be checked for proper length and angle. The rider must find the horse's best working rhythm and tempo and must help him rebalance and collect him slightly.

FIGURE 3

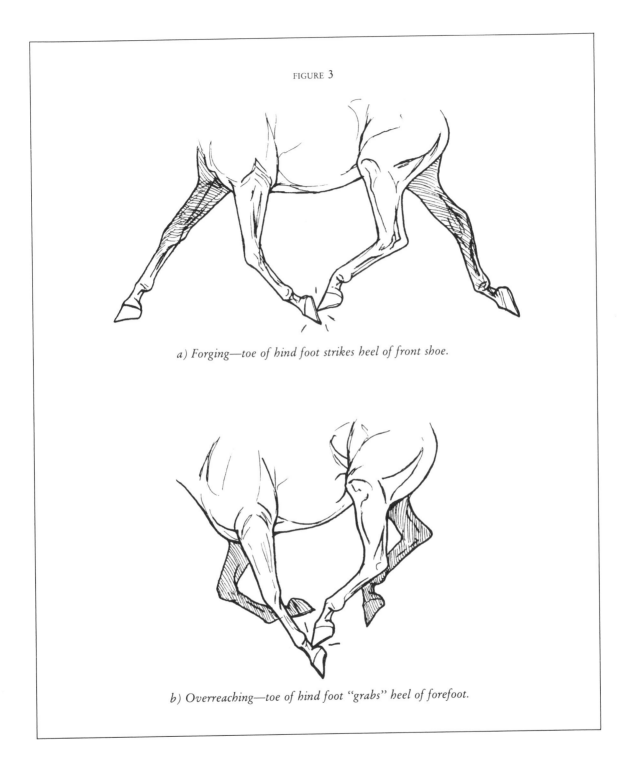

a) Forging—toe of hind foot strikes heel of front shoe.

b) Overreaching—toe of hind foot "grabs" heel of forefoot.

POOR MOVEMENT

OVERREACHING

This is an injury that happens when the horse "grabs" the heel of the forefoot with the toe of the hind foot. It may happen as a consequence of severe forging but is more common when jumping and galloping, especially in muddy, slippery or "holding" ground. If the horse's foreleg is delayed in leaving the ground, the hind foot may catch the heel as it descends. This is especially common in jumping, as the hind feet are descending just as the front feet are being picked up during the landing and recovery.

Overreaching can be prevented by keeping the feet trimmed and/or shod at a reasonable length and angle for the individual horse. Horses working or jumping in mud or slippery footing should wear protective bell boots.

8

FLEXION, BENDING AND LATERAL MOVEMENTS

People are sometimes confused by terms like "flexion," "collection," "bending," and "lateral flexion." While these are clearly defined in the dressage world, riders in other disciplines sometimes find it hard to understand what is meant by them and how they apply to their own riding, training and showing. Some trainers add to the confusion by creating their own terms (like "arcing," for bending laterally) or by changing the definition of a term to suit their own purposes. We need clear definitions that are understood and accepted by horsemen in all disciplines and that make sense when applied to any kind of horse and horse movement.

FLEXION

Flexion means "bending." Bending takes place only in joints. Flexibility is the ability to bend; the opposite is stiffness. In horse-manship, flexibility is not quite the same as suppleness, which is the ability to shift the balance easily and quickly forward, backward or sideways. While a supple horse has flexibility, flexibility alone does not create a truly supple horse.

There are two types of flexion; longitudinal (from back to front; the "long way") and lateral (sideways).

Longitudinal Flexion
(Direct Flexion)

This refers to the bending of the horse's joints from back to front, the "long way." Longitudinal flexion can refer to a part of the horse, such as flexion at the poll, neck or jaw, or to flexion throughout the whole body. "Direct flexion" usually refers more specifically to longitudinal flexion of the poll and in the mouth. When the horse flexes longitudinally in all his joints, he is said to be collected.

In collection, the horse flexes all the joints of his hind legs more (hip joints, stifles, hocks and fetlock joints) as he carries more weight on his hindquarters. The back and loins flex, especially the lumbosacral joint, and become round. (Extension of the back flattens or hollows the back.) The neck arches, raising the withers and base of the neck and lightening the forehand, and the horse flexes at the poll, bringing the head closer to a vertical position. In responding to the bridle, he flexes and relaxes his mouth and jaw, lightly chewing the bit. His forelegs bend more, moving with lighter, higher steps.

In longitudinal flexion or collection, the horse's outline becomes shorter and more compressed, with his spine rounded in a bascule. His poll reaches forward over his mouth but never in front of it, while his hind legs are engaged well forward under the body. His top line (from poll to tail) becomes longer, while his base of support shortens and his balance shifts backward.

Longitudinal flexion gives the horse contained power, like compressing a spring. He has the potential to unleash this energy in dynamic gaits, in a leap forward or upward or in movement in any direction. Staying fully collected requires great strength and is difficult to sustain for very long.

Collection must not be confused with head

FIGURE 1

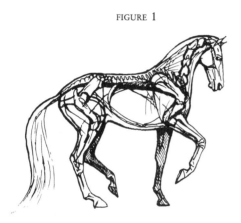

a) Longitudinal flexion or collection—flexion in all the joints

b) Energy contained in longitudinal flexion

c) Energy released in leap forward

carriage, which is the posture and angle of the head and neck. Head carriage may involve longitudinal flexion, but this may be limited to the neck and poll, without involving the rest of the horse. While the horse may arch his neck and flex at the poll until his face is vertical, this by itself does not produce the balance, engagement of the hindquarters and overall longitudinal flexion needed for true collection; in fact, his hind legs and back may be strung out and disengaged. Some horses are taught to carry their heads in a prescribed head set, which gives them a disciplined and orthodox appearance but does nothing to achieve collection. A misapplied head set can inhibit the horse's balance and movement. In true collection, head carriage is the *result* of the horse's balance and engagement, not the basis for collection.

Lateral Flexion, or Bending

The horse can flex laterally (sideways) at the poll, in the neck (which is very flexible) and very slightly in the back and lumbar spine. The croup cannot bend, but the tail is very flexible.

In order to flex laterally, the horse must flex longitudinally to some degree. Bending requires engagement of the hindquarters, lifting of the back and a slight rotation of the spinal column. Consequently there is no such thing as lateral flexion without longitudinal flexion.

In nature, horses may turn by bending in the direction of the turn, or by bending toward the outside of the turn. In an ordinary turn, the horse usually looks in the direction of the turn. When turning fast, especially when whirling or shying, horses often break into a turn shoulder first, bending to the outside, or they may turn quickly with their spine straight, without bending in either direction. Bending in the direction of the turn is associated with collection; turning without bending or bending to the outside is associated with turns at speed.

In riding, we usually prefer to have the horse bend in the direction of the turn. This allows the hind feet to track accurately behind the front feet, keeps the spinal column aligned and allows the horse to turn without leaning in. In bending, the horse engages the inside hind leg farther under the body and elevates his forehand somewhat. He also rotates his spine slightly and he shifts some of his weight from his inside shoulder to his outside shoulder. This gives him better balance in turning and in some kinds of lateral or sideways movements, especially when carrying a rider. The horse flexes his head, neck and spine in the direction of the turn, and the tail is carried slightly toward the side to which he is bent.

Bending in the opposite direction (to the outside of a turn) is called counter-bending, or outside bend. Counter-bending is called for in some training exercises, but when the horse habitually travels bent to the outside, it is a stiff and faulty movement. Turning stiffly without bending at all shows a lack of suppleness and is less comfortable for the rider.

When responding to the bit, lateral flexion should take place at the poll. The horse flexes his head slightly to the right or left at the axis joint (between the first and second cervical vertebrae). This requires relaxation in the muscles of the poll and in the mouth and jaw. The nuchal, or cervical, ligament attaches to the top of the poll. When the horse flexes correctly at the poll, this ligament slides to the side to which the horse is flexed. This causes the mane to flip toward the side of the bend. The head should be carried level, not tilted to one side, which shows a lack of true lateral flexion. Horses that bend their necks too far can evade the rider's control; this bending takes place farther back in the neck instead of at the poll and is called rubber-necking. Some horses learn to bend the neck far back near the withers and lean over one shoulder, breaking into their turns shoulder first and looking in the opposite direction. This can be caused by the rider pulling the horse sideways in an effort to restrain him.

When bending laterally, the horse should *appear* to bend evenly from his poll to his tail. Although this is not really anatomically possible, it is still the most useful image for riders, trainers and judges, because when the

FIGURE 2

a) Flexibility of the neck

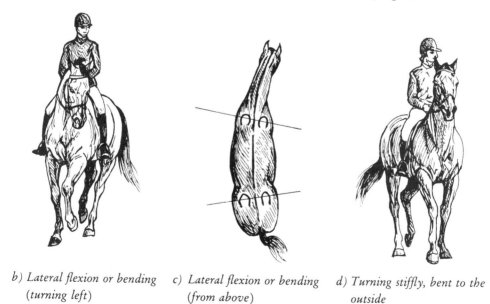

b) Lateral flexion or bending (turning left)

c) Lateral flexion or bending (from above)

d) Turning stiffly, bent to the outside

FIGURE 3

a) *Correct lateral flexion—at poll*

b) *Incorrect lateral flexion—tilted head*

c) *Incorrect lateral flexion—in neck*

horse feels and appears to be evenly bent, he moves in a coordinated and balanced turn. If the neck appears to bend more than the rest of the spine, the horse is rubbernecking, and his balance and controllability will suffer.

Some riders and trainers confuse bending with neck flexibility. A truly supple horse flexes laterally at the poll and somewhat in the neck, but his ability to bend comes more from the engagement of his inside hind leg and the lifting of his back than from bending his neck. Misguided attempts to supple a horse by pulling his mouth from side to side or tying his head around to one side are more likely to produce sore muscles, resistance and evasions like rubbernecking than true suppleness and balance in turns.

LATERAL MOVEMENTS

Lateral means "side," so lateral movements are those in which the horse moves sideways as well as forward. In nature, horses perform lateral movements when they dodge, pivot or move sideways to escape a threat or avoid an obstacle. In riding and training, lateral movements may have a practical purpose (as in opening a gate or moving out of the way of an oncoming horse or vehicle), or they may be practiced as gymnastic exercises to develop the horse's balance, suppleness and responsiveness.

Lateral movements are executed by reaching outward sideways with the forelegs and/or hind legs (abduction), and by bringing the forelegs or hind legs inward, toward and across the midline of the body (adduction). In order to move the forelegs sideways, the balance must be shifted back with some degree of collection. The spine can rotate somewhat and the shoulders and pelvis tilt to assist the legs in reaching sideways. In the forelegs, lateral movement depends on tilting the shoulder blades outward and inward; this is accomplished by the muscles at the top and side of the shoulder blade and the side of the withers, and by the muscles that run from the breastbone to the forearms. In the hind legs, the large outer muscles that run from the croup to the outside of the thigh bone move the leg outward; the deep muscles of the in-ner thigh move the leg inward. All of the muscles used in the circle of muscles are also involved when the horse moves laterally, just as they are in forward movement.

Lateral movements include certain types of turns and various sideways movements. Lateral movements executed at speed, such as the rollback of the western reining horse, are tests of agility. The lateral movements that are formalized in dressage competitions are all gymnastic exercises intended to develop the horse's strength, suppleness, responsiveness and ability to move well.

FIGURE 4

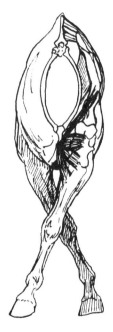

a) Abduction—reaching outward with leg

b) Adduction—reaching inward and crossing over

Lateral movements include:

Turn on the Forehand

The horse steps sideways with his hind legs in an arc around the forelegs, which remain more or less in the some place. The outside foreleg is the pivot point. The horse may bend slightly away from the direction in which the hind legs move. This and other turns may be executed as a quarter turn (90 degrees), half turn (180 degrees) or a full turn (360 degrees).

Pivot on the Hindquarters

The horse moves his forelegs sideways in an arc around the hind legs, which remain stationary. The inside hind leg is engaged farther under the body and acts as a pivot. The horse usually remains straight, but sometimes bends slightly to the outside. This turn is used primarily by western horses and may be executed slowly or at speed. When executed as a full turn (360 degrees or more) at speed, it is called a spin.

Turn on the Haunches

The horse moves his forelegs sideways in an arc around the hind legs, which remain nearly on the spot or describe a small circle. The hind legs are picked up and set down in rhythm, maintaining the pattern of the gait instead of pivoting. The horse bends evenly from poll to tail in the direction of the turn. This turn is required in dressage, where a

pivot turn would be considered a serious fault.

Turn on the Center

The horse turns around an imaginary pivot point under the center of his barrel, with the forelegs moving in the direction of the turn and the hind legs moving in the opposite direction. The horse bends in the direction of the turn. This movement allows the horse to turn in a very small space. It was practiced as a dressage movement in eighteenth-century manege riding, but is seldom used today except as a training exercise.

Side Pass (Full Pass)

The horse moves sideways, crossing his forelegs and hind legs. The foreleg and hind leg should always cross over in front of the stationary leg, never behind it, as this leads to backing up and getting stuck. The side pass is usually used by western horses, trail horses and police mounts for practical purposes such as opening a gate or crowd control; it is seldom practiced in dressage today.

Leg Yielding

The horse moves forward and sideways, crossing his forelegs and hind legs. He remains quite straight, except for a slight bend at the poll. He looks away from the direction in which he moves. Leg yielding may be practiced along the side of the arena at approximately a 35-degree angle, or on diagonal lines. It is an elementary dressage movement in which the horse learns to yield to (move away from) the riders' active leg aid, and is included in training before the horse is ready for collected work.

Shoulder-in

The horse moves forward and slightly sideways, at an angle of approximately 30 degrees to the track. His forehand is carried slightly to the inside, and he is evenly bent from poll to tail away from the direction in which he moves. When viewed from the front, his legs move on three tracks—the outside hind leg moves on the outer track, the outside foreleg and inside hind leg move on the center track and the inside foreleg moves on the inner track. The shoulder-in requires increased engagement of the inside hind leg and lifting of the back, with a lowering of the inside haunch. When performed with the horse using his body well, it develops the horse's engagement, suppleness, straightness and ability to carry himself in his best balance. It can be performed on straight lines or on a circle.

Haunches-in (Travers)

The horse moves forward and slightly sideways, at approximately a 30-degree angle to the track. His front legs move straight along the track, with the hind legs carried slightly to the inside. The horse is evenly bent from poll to tail in the direction in which he is traveling. The haunches-in increases the engagement of

the inside hind leg and is useful in developing the ability of the hindquarters to carry more of the horse's weight in collection. It can be performed on straight lines or on a circle.

Renvers (Haunches-out)

This is the inverse of the haunches-in, or travers. It is performed similarly to the haunches-in, except that the tail is toward the wall and the head is toward the inside of the arena. The horse moves in the direction toward which he is bent.

Half-pass (Two Tracks)

This is a variation of the haunches-in, or travers, which is executed on a diagonal line instead of along the wall. The horse moves forward and sideways, slightly bent around the rider's inside leg and looking in the direction in which he is moving. The outside forelegs and hind legs cross over in front of the inside legs. The horse's body should be parallel to the long side of the arena, but his forehand should be slightly in advance of his hindquarters. It is important for the horse to maintain the same cadence, balance and correct bend throughout the movement, and that his inside hind leg is well engaged for every stride.

The half-pass is sometimes confused with leg yielding, which it superficially resembles. However, leg yielding is an elementary movement in which the horse is straight, looking slightly away from the direction in which he moves, while the half-pass is a

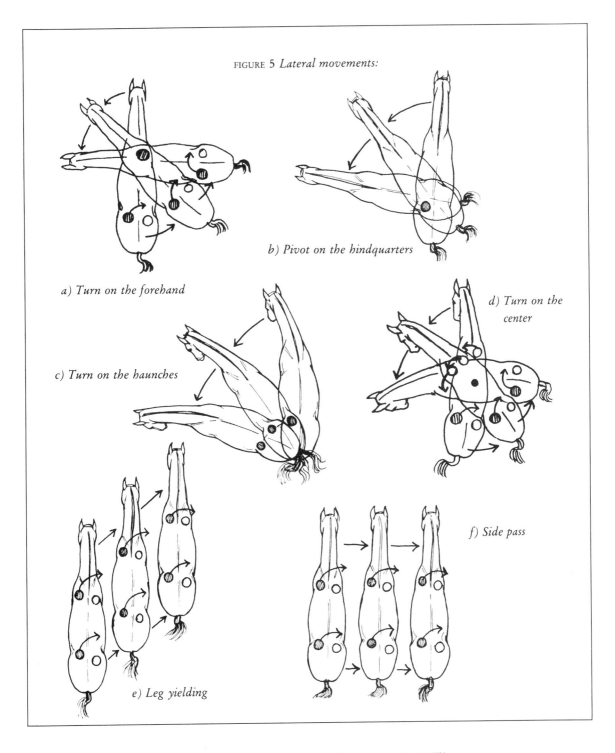

FIGURE 5 *Lateral movements:*

b) Pivot on the hindquarters

a) Turn on the forehand

d) Turn on the center

c) Turn on the haunches

f) Side pass

e) Leg yielding

FLEXION, BENDING AND LATERAL MOVEMENTS

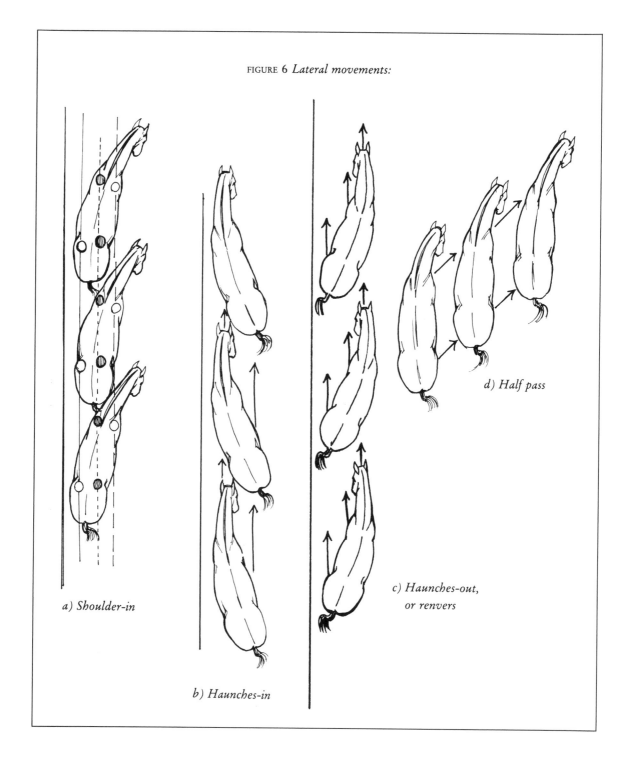

FIGURE 6 *Lateral movements:*

a) Shoulder-in

b) Haunches-in

c) Haunches-out,
or renvers

d) Half pass

much more advanced movement which requires a greater degree of suppleness, collection and engagement, with the horse bending in the direction in which he moves.

When a horse makes repeated half-passes of several strides alternating to the left and right in a zigzag pattern, it is called a counterchange of hand.

There are many other variations of lateral movements. All are gymnastic exercises that use and develop certain muscles and improve the horse's ability to collect himself and move fluently forward and sideways.

In lateral work, it is important to remember that basic gait qualities such as rhythm, relaxation, engagement and good use of the horse's mechanism must come first. Lateral work must be correctly executed in order to improve the horse's way of going. If the horse is cranked into an unnatural attitude and forced to move sideways, the lateral movements will be awkward, ugly and damaging to the horse's movement; they may cause strain and injury as well.

9

TYPES OF MOVEMENT

Different breeds and types of horses exhibit characteristic types or styles of movement. The type of movement that is desired depends on the job the horse is required to do and sometimes on movement characteristics that are prized in his particular breed. The *type* of movement should not be confused with the *quality* of the movement—any type of movement can be performed well or poorly, and no one type of movement is superior to another. However, a horse that moves with an inappropriate type of movement for the purpose he is used for is handicapped in his performance and will be discriminated against in showing, no matter how well he moves in his own way.

TYPES OF MOVEMENT

Types of movement can be characterized by the horse's action and balance:

Long, Low Movement

Characterized by long, low strides and efficient ground-covering action, sometimes called "daisy-cutting" action. The legs swing forward from the hip and shoulder with little flexion in the knees and hocks and appear fairly straight as they move. This kind of movement exhibits extension and forward movement well, but is less suited for highly collected gaits and movements with great suspension. Typical of Thoroughbreds, hunters and horses of Thoroughbred type.

Short, Low Movement

Characterized by low strides with little flexion at the knees and hocks but with a short stride. The horse may engage his hind legs and can turn, stop and work off his hocks handily, but his neck and head are low and extended and he remains in a basically forward balance. Typical of western horses, especially the old-style Quarter Horse type.

Round Movement

Characterized by a rounded stride with forward reach and flexion of the knees and hocks. The movement is both ground-covering and upward, but not as extreme as high action. The action must be balanced, with the flexion of the hocks equal to that of the knees. The gait gives the impression of a wheel. Typical of Morgans and some other pleasure riding and driving horses.

High Action

Characterized by elevated action with great animation and energy. The horse moves in a collected balance with a high head carriage and marked flexion of the knees and hocks; the forearms may be brought up past the horizontal, and the legs are folded tightly. The action is more up and down than forward, particularly in the hind legs. Some gaits are performed at speed, but without sacrificing form or high action. Typical of Hackneys, American Saddlebreds and Park horses of other breeds.

Medium Movement

Characterized by long, ground-covering strides that exhibit some bend in the joints and elevation. Knee and hock flexion is evident but not extreme. The strides have some arch and elevation, but are long and flowing.

This type of movement may show brilliant extended gaits and can achieve good collection as well. Typical of European Warmbloods, but may be found in some Arabians, Morgans and individuals of other breeds.

Baroque Movement

Characterized by high, round and elastic strides with much suspension. The joints of the legs are flexed more than in medium movement, although not to the extreme of high action. The horse moves in a collected balance and may show talent for the passage, piaffe and other highly collected gaits, although limited in speed and extension. Baroque movement is so named because it was characteristic of the manege horses of the seventeenth century; today it is typical of Lippizaners and Andalusians.

MOVEMENT FOR DIFFERENT TYPES OF PERFORMANCE

The best type of movement for a certain purpose is determined by the job the horse performs and the most functional and efficient movement for that job. Appropriate movement for the major types of performance horses in North America today follows:

Hunter and Jumper Movement

The hunter, whether in the hunting field or show ring, should move with long, low and ground-covering strides and a free, fluid way

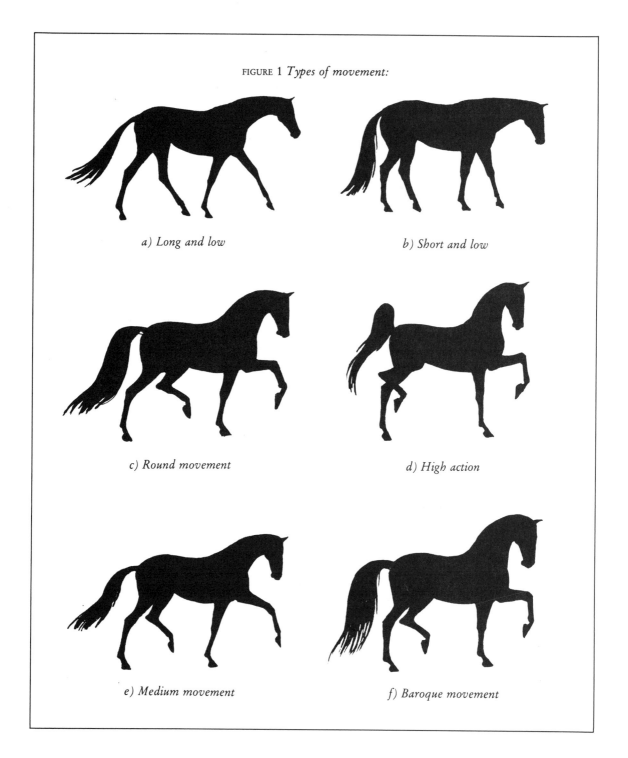

FIGURE 1 *Types of movement:*

a) Long and low

b) Short and low

c) Round movement

d) High action

e) Medium movement

f) Baroque movement

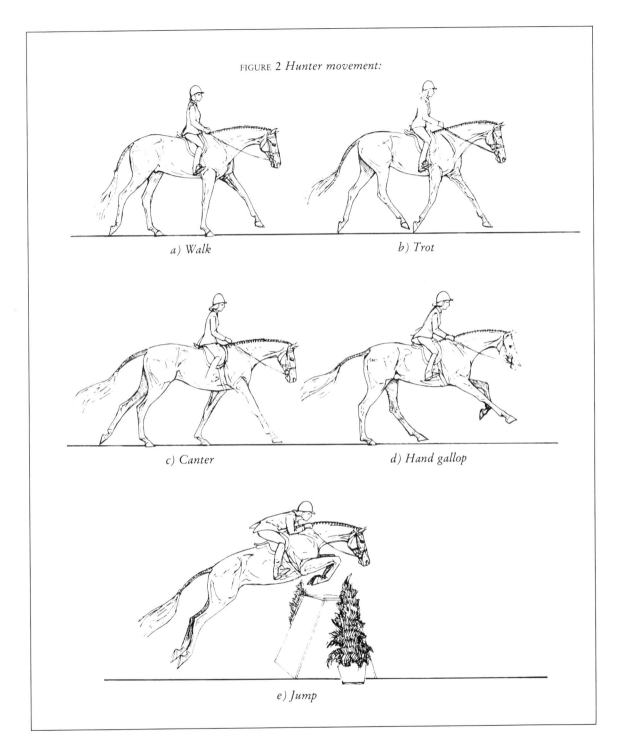

FIGURE 2 *Hunter movement:*

a) Walk

b) Trot

c) Canter

d) Hand gallop

e) Jump

TYPES OF MOVEMENT

of going. His action should be smooth and efficient, pointing his toes and floating over the ground without excessive knee action or short, choppy strides. His balance is moderately forward, to facilitate galloping and jumping. He should always look and feel well balanced and be able to cope with jumping and turning and with rolling terrain and natural ground conditions. His attitude should be calm but alert, mannerly and responsive; his head carriage is moderately extended, but he will collect smoothly in transitions. When asked to extend his stride, a good hunter remains in rhythm and lengthens his stride without quickening his tempo. He has a free, reaching and ground-covering walk with good engagement; a flowing, regular and well-balanced trot and a moderately collected canter. His gallop is long striding but well balanced and mannerly. Working hunters are judged on their ability to maintain an even hunting pace and to jump in stride in good form without speeding up, slowing down or hesitation.

Faults in hunter type movement would include: rough or high action; short or restricted strides; moving too much on the forehand, behind the bit or over-collected; stiff or inverted movement; rushing, lazy or inconsistent gaits. High action, baroque or round movement is inappropriate.

Jumpers are judged only on their performance, not on their movement. Good jumpers often exhibit some of the characteristics of good hunter movement, but many show rounder, more collected movement than would be ideal for a hunter. Some successful

FIGURE 2-A *Faulty hunter movement:*

a) *Short, high and choppy movement*

b) *"Strung out"; too much on the forehand*

c) *Overbent; on the forehand and forging*

jumpers have had round action, which gives them the ability to fold their legs over fences and sometimes the ability to jump high, but this type of movement does not favor speed or scope as much as medium movement.

Successful event horses usually have either long and low or medium movement. They need efficient, ground-covering strides and speed for cross-country work, but must be able to jump with power, scope and agility and must produce correct gaits and movement for dressage. Round, high or baroque movement does not produce the speed necessary for a top-level event horse; most of the best move long and low.

Movement for Dressage

While dressage work, properly applied, can help to improve any horse, not all horses are equally suitable for competitive dressage, especially at the upper levels. The ideal dressage horse must have three correct and pure gaits, free from faults like pacing in the walk or a four-beat canter. Although there have been excellent performers at top levels who showed long and low, round and baroque movement, current trends tend to favor the horse with medium movement for dressage competition. Some high-level riders who are more concerned with the art of dressage than competition favor the baroque type. High action and short and low movement are inappropriate.

A dressage horse needs good balance, freedom of movement, lively impulsion and true, straight movement. Correct engagement is essential, as this is the basis for balance, collection and all movement. Rhythm is most important, and a horse that moves with natural suspension and elastic, cadenced movement has a natural advantage.

The walk should be regular, with good engagement and overstep and four clean, evenly spaced beats. A tendency to pace in the walk is a serious fault. The trot should be regular, cadenced and elastic, with freedom of movement and good balance. There must be two clean beats with suspension. The ability to engage the hind legs well and move with scope and good suspension shows promise for dressage. (A flashy but incorrect extended trot, performed with the back hollow and the hocks trailing but with exaggerated extension of the forelegs, sometimes leads inexperienced judges to conclude that this horse would make a great dressage horse—in reality, the horse could have limited potential and would be difficult to train.) The canter should be elastic and well balanced and should have three clean beats with a definite moment of suspension or "jump." A stiff, flat canter with little suspension or a lateral canter that resembles a pace would handicap the horse in collected canter work, good extensions and clean flying changes.

The most important characteristic of good dressage movement is good engagement of the hind legs and hindquarters, resulting in the horse moving with a good bascule. Hind legs that are stiff and cannot bend well, lazy hind legs that do not reach forward or hind legs that swing out behind the horse more than they reach forward cannot produce the best gaits for dressage. Extremely high action

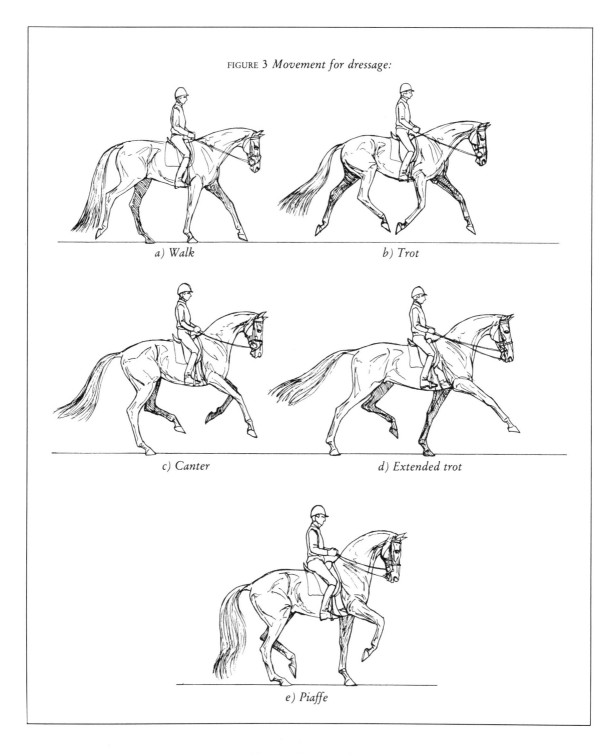

FIGURE 3 *Movement for dressage:*

a) Walk

b) Trot

c) Canter

d) Extended trot

e) Piaffe

in the hind legs is not desirable, as it often goes with a stiff back and a lack of true engagement.

The dressage horse must work on the bit, especially in higher-level work; a round, elastic back and the ability to raise the withers and the base of the neck are essential to his balance and an effective connection with the bit.

Western Gaits and Movement

The western horse works with low and efficient strides with little hock and knee flexion. He may move with short, low strides (more characteristic of the older type of Quarter Horse) or with long, low strides (more typical of the modern Quarter Horse that is closer to the Thoroughbred in build and movement). Certain breeds such as the Arabian and Morgan, which exhibit round or medium movement, may also be ridden and shown western. High action and baroque movement are inappropriate except in parade horses.

Western gaits should be relaxed, free and easy and unconstrained; the horse's balance is moderately forward, but he engages his hind legs and works off his hocks. Excessive speed is penalized. His head carriage is moderately low and extended, with the neck carried near the level of the back. His head is carried relaxed and flexed at the poll, with his face approaching the vertical. The western horse works on a loose rein or a light rein (a rein that sags slightly between the rider's hand and the bit); he should not need excessive restraint.

There are two primary styles within western riding: the split-rein style, originating in Texas and the Midwest, and the California style, which evolved from the Spanish vaqueros. The split-rein style favors a longer rein and a lower, more extended head carriage and usually employs mild curb bits such as grazing bits.

The California style employs closed (romal) reins and half-breed or spade bits and produces a more collected horse with a slightly more elevated carriage. The split-rein style is often used with Quarter Horses and horses that move short and low, although it is also appropriate for longer-striding horses. The California style is often favored by riders of Arabians, Morgans and other breeds that exhibit medium or rounded movement and present a better picture when quite collected. It can also be used to advantage on longer-striding horses, particularly when they require more collection to show at their best. Both styles are acceptable throughout the country, although there are some local preferences.

The basic gaits of the western horse are the walk, jog, lope and gallop. The walk is free moving but unhurried, engaging the hind legs well. The jog is slow, smooth and easy, with a relaxed back and little suspension; it should retain two clean beats without breaking into a four-beat shuffle. The lope is slow, unconstrained and elastic, with three clean beats. A four-beat lope shows that the horse is uncoordinated and on the forehand and is a serious fault; it is often seen when the horse is made to lope more slowly than he can move

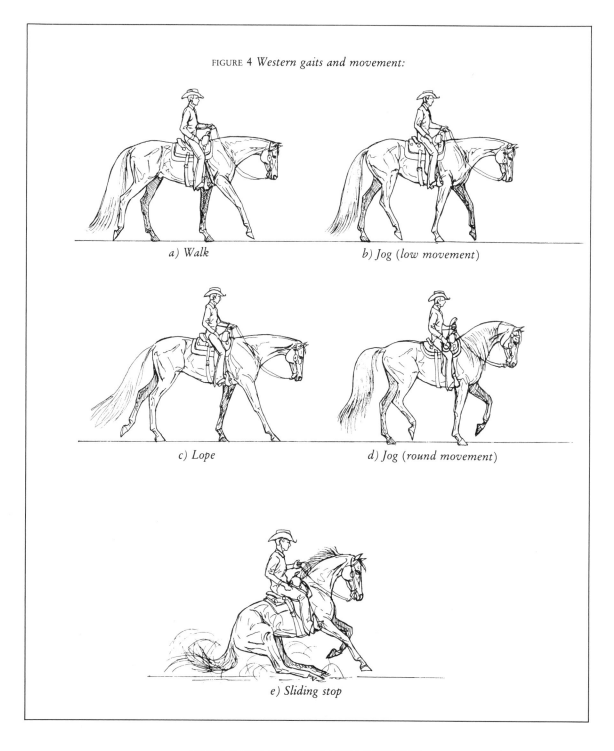

FIGURE 4 *Western gaits and movement:*

a) Walk

b) Jog (low movement)

c) Lope

d) Jog (round movement)

e) Sliding stop

well. All western gaits must be performed on a loose or light rein without unnecessary restraint.

Western performance horses adopt a more collected attitude when working, especially when performing a reining pattern. The working lope and gallop show more impulsion, but the horse should remain calm and responsive on a light rein. Western movements and transitions are made all at once rather than progressively; the horse engages his hind legs and stops on his hindquarters in one motion instead of taking a few steps at the trot or walk before stopping. The horse should move out at speed willingly when called upon, but he is always balanced and alert to the rider so that he can stop or turn instantly.

Major faults in western horses' movement would include rough gaits, excessive speed, high action, high head or inverted frame, inconsistent rhythm, breaking up the clean rhythm of the gait (shuffling in the jog or four-beat lope) and working excessively on the forehand.

English Pleasure Gaits and Movement

The pleasure horse or pony may be of any breed or type, but he should be stylish, pleasant and comfortable to ride. The gaits should be smooth, balanced and collected. The preferred type of movement for pleasure horses is medium or round movement, which is often found in Arabians, Morgans and other typical pleasure breeds. Long and low movement is acceptable and is preferred for the hunter-type pleasure horse, but short and low movement is less desirable. Baroque movement is acceptable but less usual. Within the high-actioned breeds, such as the American Saddlebred and Walking Horse, there are classes for pleasure horses whose action is less extreme and easier to ride; these horses are shown as Country Pleasure Horses, Plantation Pleasure Horses or Show Pleasure Horses. Many versatile pleasure horses drive, jump or ride western as well as English.

English pleasure horses and hacks are ridden in a collected balance, which produces smooth, balanced gaits that are easy to ride. In most American shows the typical English pleasure horse is ridden Saddle Seat. Hunter type pleasure horses and ponies and hunter hacks (which are required to jump two low fences) are ridden hunter seat. A road hack is a pleasure horse with stylish gaits and ground-covering action; he must be capable of extending the trot and canter and is ridden Saddle Seat. The gaits of the pleasure horse are the walk, trot and canter. Some pleasure horses are asked to extend the trot, and certain classes may be asked for a hand gallop. The walk should be regular, elastic and ground-covering, engaging the hind legs well. The trot should be balanced, regular and elastic, with somewhat collected balance and free movement. The canter should be collected, smooth and straight on both leads, with three clean beats and a gentle, elastic movement. When asked to extend a gait, the horse should remain in balance and lengthen his stride without quickening his tempo. A pleasure horse must respond smoothly in transitions, should stand quietly and should back straight and promptly. In harness, pleasure driving horses perform a walk, a pleasure trot (slightly collected trot) and a road trot or strong trot (extended trot but without extreme speed).

Pleasure horses are usually ridden on light contact or on a light (slightly loose) rein. They must remain in self-carriage and respond willingly to light aids. Strong contact is inappropriate, and excessive speed is penalized. Extremely loose reins are not recommended and often result in a strung-out horse that moves sloppily.

Faulty movement for a pleasure horse would include stiff, rough or choppy gaits; inconsistent rhythm and balance; too fast or too slow; inverted frame, above the bit; behind the bit; short or restricted strides; on the forehand or heavy in hand; crooked or sideways movement; rough or unbalanced transitions; failure to back straight and readily.

Gaits and Movement for Gaited Saddle Horses or Park Horses

Park horses, three- and five-gaited saddle horses and show walking horses must show elegance, animation and high action. They are ridden in collected balance with a high head carriage and great elevation of the knees and hocks. High action is essential and is cultivated by training, special shoeing and sometimes by artificial action devices such as light chains, or "rattlers," around the pasterns.

Long and low, short and low or baroque movement is unsuitable, and medium or round movement is insufficient when compared with correct high action.

The saddle horse's walk is the "animated walk," which may be a collected four-beat walk with high action or a slow jog with high steps. The trot is collected, balanced and brilliant, with the knees and hocks highly flexed. The horse must move in form with balanced action—that is, his knee flexion must be proportionate to his hock flexion. He must not "promise more in front than he delivers behind." The canter is collected and elevated with high action; it should not be too fast.

The five-gaited horse performs the rack and slow gait in addition to the three gaits; the horse must show balance, form and rhythm at the slow gait and should rack at speed without sacrificing form. The Tennessee Walking Horse performs an animated flat walk, a fast running walk with high action and a collected canter. The extremely high action and reach of the show walking horse at the running walk is called the "big lick." Show walking horses elevate their forehands at the canter, resulting in a four-beat "rocking-chair" canter. Both types must make clean transitions from one gait to another without pacing or mixing gaits.

Faulty saddle horse movement would include rough, short or low action; leaning or lugging on the bit; mixing gaits or a tendency to pace; insufficient collection or animation; labored action; sprawling, dragging hocks or going wide behind; unbalanced action (higher action in the front legs than in the hind legs).

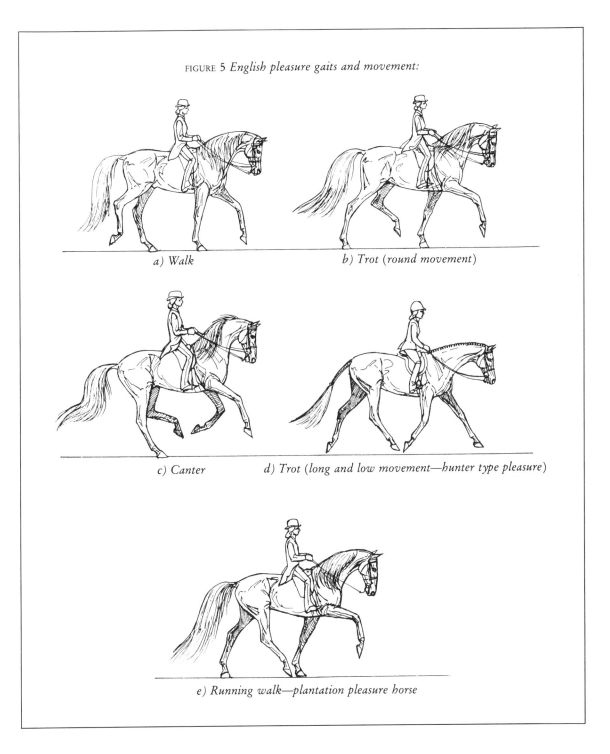

FIGURE 5 *English pleasure gaits and movement:*

a) Walk

b) Trot (round movement)

c) Canter

d) Trot (long and low movement—hunter type pleasure)

e) Running walk—plantation pleasure horse

TYPES OF MOVEMENT

113

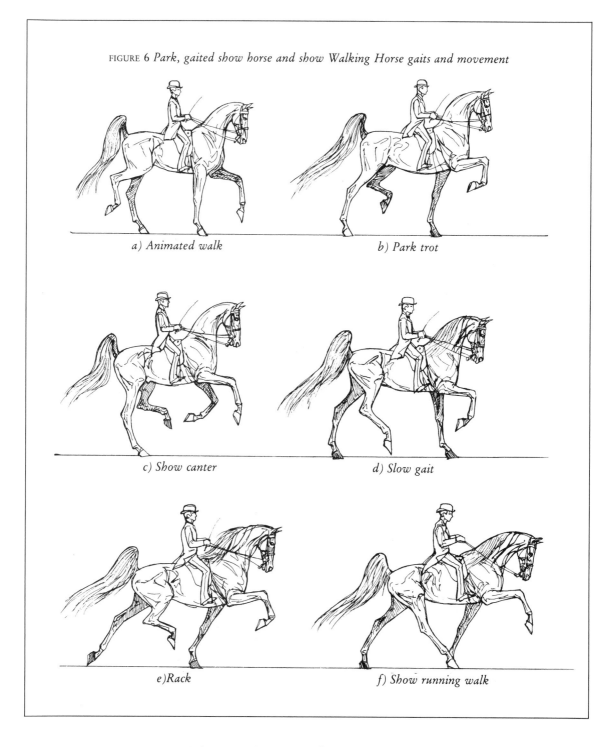

FIGURE 6 *Park, gaited show horse and show Walking Horse gaits and movement*

a) Animated walk

b) Park trot

c) Show canter

d) Slow gait

e) Rack

f) Show running walk

HORSE GAITS, BALANCE AND MOVEMENT

10

CONFORMATION AND MOVEMENT

Conformation, or the way a horse is built, determines the kind of movement he is capable of. While some conformation points may be merely aesthetic (such as the size of the ears or the shape of the head), most are functional. When selecting a horse to move well, we should evaluate key conformation points that directly affect movement. When judging horses in conformation classes, functional conformation that produces good movement should be preferred over mere prettiness or the "look" that happens to be popular at the moment.

A detailed analysis of conformation and its relationship to movement could fill a volume, so only some of the most important conformation points will be covered here.

PROPORTION AND BALANCE

The parts of the horse should appear to be in proportion to each other, and the horse should appear balanced. A horse that appears heavy in the forequarters and light behind is likely to move on the forehand. A horse with short legs will not move with long, flowing strides, and a horse built with his hips higher than his withers will have difficulty in collection.

HEAD AND NECK

The horse's head and neck are his "balancer"; an especially large head is more difficult to balance than a smaller one. The way the head articulates with the neck and the way the neck is set into the body help to determine the horse's balance, natural carriage and way of responding to the bridle. The jaws should

FIGURE 1

a) Good proportions and balance

b) Poor proportions and balance

a higher-set neck (which rises up from the shoulders) makes collection and high action easier. A ewe neck dips on the top and bulges underneath; it tends to produce a high head and an inverted frame and makes flexion at the poll difficult. A bull neck (short, thick and heavy neck) goes with short strides and a tendency to be heavy in hand.

SHOULDER

The angle of the shoulder blade determines the range of motion and length of stride of the foreleg. (To find the angle of the shoulder, look from the point of the shoulder along the ridge of the scapula.) A sloping shoulder rotates farther back and allows the foreleg to reach farther forward and upward (an important consideration in jumpers). A straight shoulder restricts the range of motion and the length of the stride, but favors high knee action. An upright shoulder angle also produces more concussion and a rougher gait than a more sloping shoulder.

be wide enough to allow the horse to flex comfortably without squeezing the windpipe; a thick throttle or narrow jaws can inhibit flexion at the poll.

A long neck favors a long stride because the long muscles of the neck help to draw the foreleg forward. A low-set neck (one that comes out of the front of the chest) goes with forward balance and moving on the forehand;

FORELEG PROPORTIONS

The relative length of the bones of the foreleg affects the length of the stride and the type of movement. The ideal proportions are long shoulder, short arm, long forearm, short cannon and medium pastern. These proportions give a longer, freer stride with a greater range of motion and less stress on the tendons and

FIGURE 2

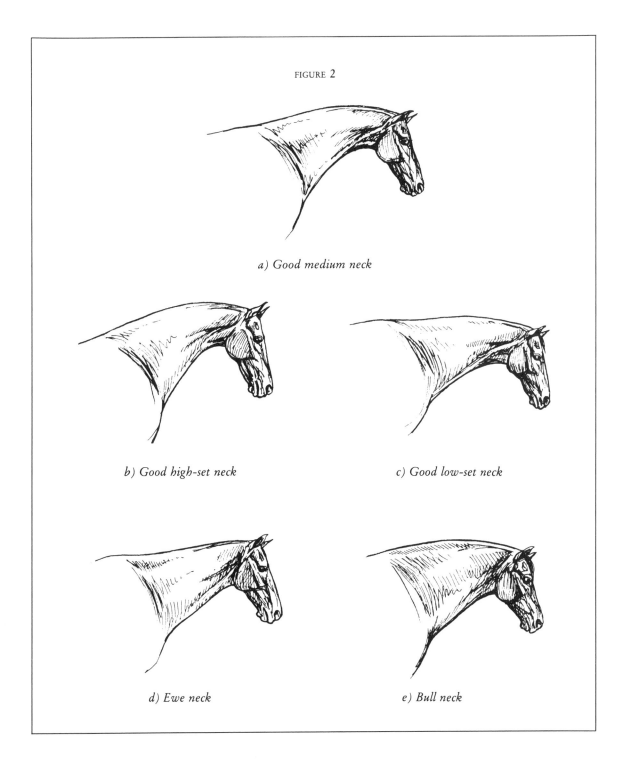

a) Good medium neck

b) Good high-set neck

c) Good low-set neck

d) Ewe neck

e) Bull neck

CONFORMATION AND MOVEMENT

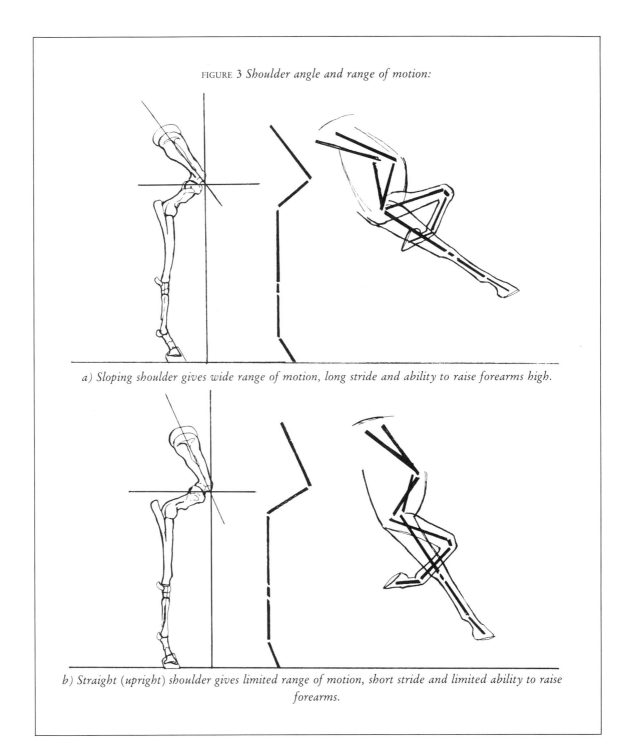

FIGURE 3 *Shoulder angle and range of motion:*

a) Sloping shoulder gives wide range of motion, long stride and ability to raise forearms high.

b) Straight (upright) shoulder gives limited range of motion, short stride and limited ability to raise forearms.

structures of the lower leg. A short shoulder, long arm, short forearm and long cannon produce a shorter stride and put the tendons and ligaments under more stress.

Pasterns absorb shock and should be of medium length and slope. The longer and more sloping the pastern, the smoother the ride; however, very long and sloping pasterns are more prone to breaking down. A short pastern is stronger but does not absorb shock as well as a longer pastern; an upright pastern results in rough gaits. Short, upright pasterns are the worst conformation; they create short, rough gaits with excessive concussion for both horse and rider.

HINDQUARTERS

If the pelvis is long and the hindquarters deep and wide, the large hindquarter muscles will be long and well developed and the horse can move with more power. Good length from the point of the hip to the point of the buttock and from hip joint to stifle is desirable. Viewed from the rear, a well-rounded croup shows good development of the important hamstring group, and a horse that is wide and well developed through the stifles has large and strong hamstring, quadricep and rectus femoris muscles.

A tipped pelvis can be powerful if it is long and well muscled, but it goes with a longer back and loin. A short, steep croup with a short pelvis is a weak hindquarter. A very flat croup may place the hind legs far back, making it difficult for the horse to engage his hind legs.

HIND LEG PROPORTIONS AND ANGLES

The hind legs are levers that move the horse. A long line from hip to hock permits a long stride with better engagement of the hind leg. This goes with short hind cannons and hocks well let down (close to the ground), which is a more powerful conformation. Longer hind cannons favor higher action and more flexion in the hocks, but they are not as strong. The hind pasterns are usually somewhat more upright than the front pasterns, but they should still be of medium length and slope. Very long, sloping hind pasterns are weak and are prone to running down (striking the ground with the back of the fetlock joint).

The angles at the hip joint, stifle joint and hock determine the placement of the hind leg under the hindquarters, which is important for power, ability to engage the hindquarters and length of stride. The ideal hind leg is placed so that a vertical line dropped from the point of the buttock would run down the back of the hock and the lower leg. A vertical line down the center of the cannon bone would just touch the back of the heel. This placement gives good, average angles at hip joint, stifle, hock and pastern.

Excessively straight hind legs are called post legs. They engage by swinging forward with little flexion, a configuration that is good for speed but makes collection and "sitting on the hocks" difficult. Sickle hocks are hocks that are always slightly bent; they place the hind leg forward under the body but are prone to strain and may develop curbs. Sickle

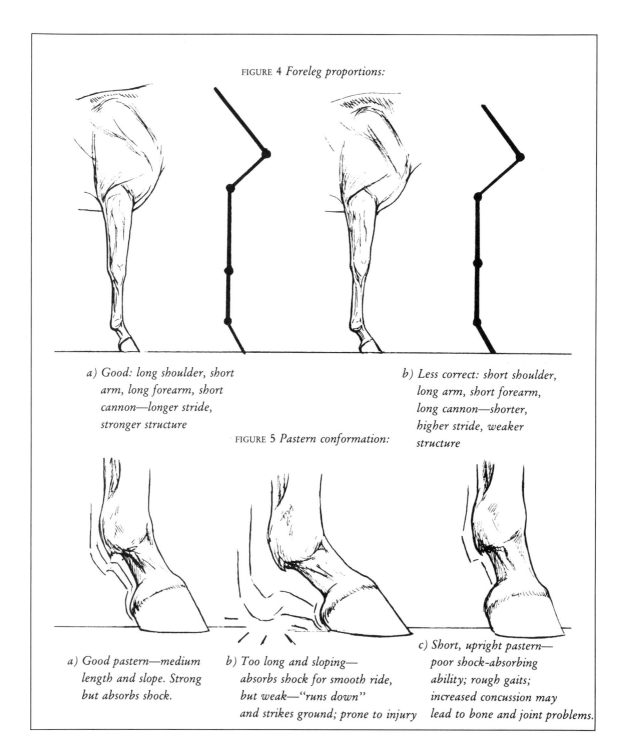

FIGURE 4 *Foreleg proportions:*

a) Good: long shoulder, short arm, long forearm, short cannon—longer stride, stronger structure

b) Less correct: short shoulder, long arm, short forearm, long cannon—shorter, higher stride, weaker structure

FIGURE 5 *Pastern conformation:*

a) Good pastern—medium length and slope. Strong but absorbs shock.

b) Too long and sloping— absorbs shock for smooth ride, but weak—"runs down" and strikes ground; prone to injury

c) Short, upright pastern— poor shock-absorbing ability; rough gaits; increased concussion may lead to bone and joint problems.

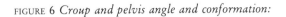

FIGURE 6 *Croup and pelvis angle and conformation:*

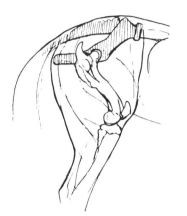

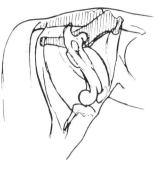

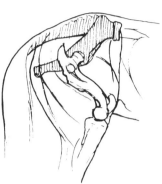

a) Good pelvis, croup and hindquarter conformation

b) Flat croup and pelvis

c) Tipped croup and pelvis

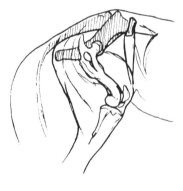

d) Short, steep croup and pelvis—weak "goose rump"

e) Good pelvis, croup and hindquarter conformation (from rear)

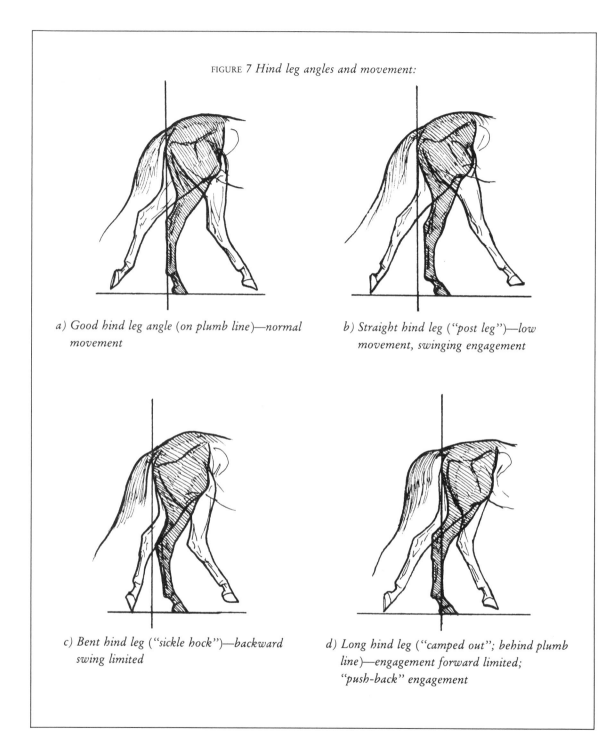

FIGURE 7 *Hind leg angles and movement:*

a) *Good hind leg angle (on plumb line)—normal movement*

b) *Straight hind leg ("post leg")—low movement, swinging engagement*

c) *Bent hind leg ("sickle hock")—backward swing limited*

d) *Long hind leg ("camped out"; behind plumb line)—engagement forward limited; "push-back" engagement*

FIGURE 8 *Hind leg proportions:*

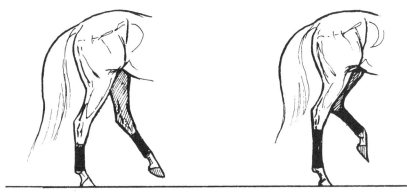

a) Long line from hip to hock; hocks "well let down"; short cannon—long, powerful stride

b) Shorter line from hip to hock; hocks higher; long cannon—higher, shorter stride

hocks favor collected gaits but are not designed for great speed. Hocks that are camped out (placed too far back) make it difficult for the horse to engage his hind legs; he will be weak behind and prone to move on the forehand.

LEG ALIGNMENT FROM FRONT AND REAR

The ideal leg conformation is straight and symmetrical; a vertical line dropped from the point of the shoulder should fall down the center of the leg and hoof all the way to the ground. Toeing out causes the horse to "wing in"—the leg swings inward and may interfere, striking the opposite leg. Toeing in causes the horse to "paddle"—the leg swings outward. A base-narrow horse is wider above than at the feet; he may "rope-walk," placing one foot in front of the other. A base-wide horse is narrow above and wide below, which usually indicates poor muscle development.

In the hind legs, the cannons should be vertical and parallel, but the stifles and toes normally point somewhat outward. This permits the stifles to engage far forward without bumping against the belly. The feet should point outward at the same angle as the stifles to avoid stress on the joints. Cow hocks are crooked hocks; the hocks point inward while the cannon bones angle outward. Bowed hocks are the opposite; the hocks point out and the cannon bones angle inward. Both are weaker than normal hocks and rotate as the horse moves; this causes grinding stress to the bones of the hock and may lead to hock ailments such as spavin. Hind legs that are placed close together, but with the cannon

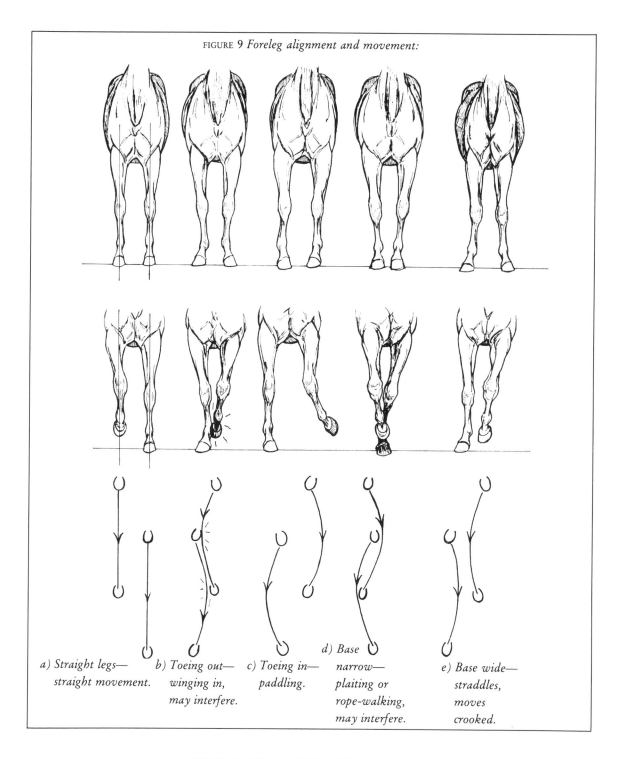

FIGURE 9 *Foreleg alignment and movement:*

a) *Straight legs— straight movement.*

b) *Toeing out— winging in, may interfere.*

c) *Toeing in— paddling.*

d) *Base narrow— plaiting or rope-walking, may interfere.*

e) *Base wide— straddles, moves crooked.*

HORSE GAITS, BALANCE AND MOVEMENT

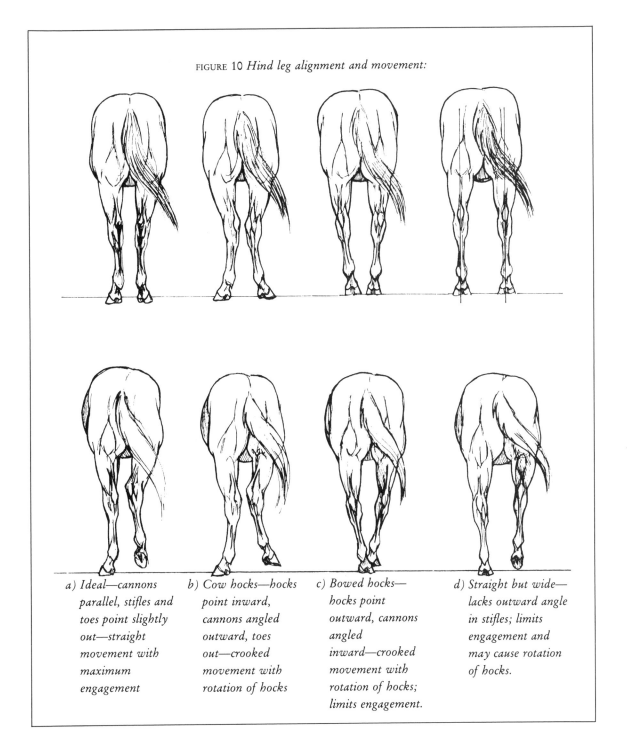

FIGURE 10 *Hind leg alignment and movement:*

a) Ideal—cannons parallel, stifles and toes point slightly out—straight movement with maximum engagement

b) Cow hocks—hocks point inward, cannons angled outward, toes out—crooked movement with rotation of hocks

c) Bowed hocks—hocks point outward, cannons angled inward—crooked movement with rotation of hocks; limits engagement.

d) Straight but wide—lacks outward angle in stifles; limits engagement and may cause rotation of hocks.

bones vertical and parallel, should not be confused with cow hocks. This conformation places the hind legs more nearly under the horse's center of gravity and may contribute to better balance and use of the hind legs. It gives better balance and power than hind legs placed excessively wide apart.

THE BACK: SHAPE AND PROPORTIONS

The back is the "transmission" between the hindquarters and the forehand; it also carries the rider, so it is one of the most important conformation factors in movement. The lumbosacral joint is a key area in the back, as this is where engagement of the hindquarters is determined. The loin should be broad, strongly muscled and not too long; this makes for a strong lumbar region. The coupling (lumbosacral joint) and croup should be well muscled and slightly rounded. A rough coupling points to lack of muscle de-

velopment and sometimes to an awkward angle of the lumbar spine to the sacrum and pelvis. A protuberance at the coupling may be a "jumper's bump"—a swelling caused by partial dislocation of the lumbosacral joint at some time, which can happen when a horse makes a severe effort with both hind legs. (Some horses have an especially high coupling even if they have not been injured.) A long back makes it more difficult for the horse to collect himself and shift his balance, but some length to the back seems to favor scope and amplitude of movement. A short back usually means a handy horse, but some very short-backed horses are not as smooth and springy in their movement as longer-backed horses.

A roach back is one that is rounded upward; it is hard to fit a saddle and can make it difficult for the horse to use his back in a coordinated effort to lighten the forehand. A hollow back (sway back) makes it even more difficult for the horse to collect himself or to transmit power from the hindquarters

FIGURE 11 *Loin and coupling conformation:*

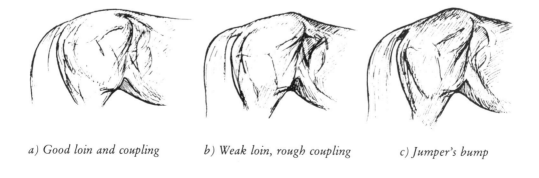

a) Good loin and coupling   *b) Weak loin, rough coupling*   *c) Jumper's bump*

FIGURE 12 *Back conformation:*

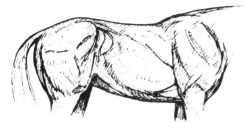

a) Good back, loin and croup

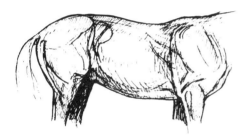

b) Roach back

c) Hollow back

through the back. A hollow back may be a congenital condition, but it is more often the result of uncoordinated and inverted movement.

The withers should lie well back and should be clean and of moderate height. Since the back and neck muscles attach to the spines of the withers, short, low withers give less space and length for muscles and are associated with short, stubby gaits and moving on the forehand. Extremely high, sharp withers may simply indicate a lack of muscle development, but they may also show that the shoulders are short and steep.

"Mutton withers," which appear to be flat or buried in fat, along with broad, fat and "loaded" shoulders, often go with a short, thick neck and a broad chest. This conformation tends to make the horse ride heavy in hand, and he may have a tendency to roll from side to side as he moves.

Certain conformation points are characteristic of some breeds or of horses that move with a certain type of action. What may be considered a fault in one breed may be a bonus for another type of horse. For instance, Tennessee Walking Horses often have a low-set croup or tipped pelvis, which facilitates the reach of the hind legs in the running walk; good jumpers often have a straight hind leg and may have a rounded croup or a "jumper's bump." A good western horse may have heavier hindquarter muscling and shorter forelegs than would be acceptable in a high-actioned saddle horse. A slight tendency to "stand under" in the hind legs, which would be a fault in a Saddlebred, might help a working stock horse to "get into the ground" in a sliding stop. It is important to learn the characteristics that favor good movement and are functional in a particular breed or type of performance horse. These should be considered when selecting a prospect to train or in judging conformation classes.

This chapter has only touched on some of the basics of conformation in relation to movement. For a more detailed discussion, see Deb Bennett, *Principles of Conformation Analysis* (Fleet Street Publishing Corp., 1989) vols. I, II and III.

11

SHOEING AND MOVEMENT

Trimming and shoeing can have a profound effect, for better or for worse, on the way a horse moves. In nature, horses wear their feet into a shape that reflects their conformation, their natural movement and the terrain they live on. When we ride horses, we must trim or shoe their feet to keep them sound and able to function at their best.

Horses often need help in some way from shoeing and/or trimming. The feet may grow out until the toes are too long or the hoof angle is incorrect, making the horse likely to trip or injure himself if the feet are not trimmed to a more normal angle. Some horses wear their hoofs down until they become tender and sore-footed; they need shoes for protection. When working on some surfaces, shoeing gives the horse security by providing traction and preventing slipping. Some horses need special shoeing to help correct a faulty way of going or to protect a weak or damaged foot or leg. Special shoeing may be used to accentuate a style of moving (such as high action) or to refine and develop a particular gait.

As each leg moves, it goes through an arc or flight path. The hoof "breaks over" the toe as it leaves the ground. During the first half of the flight, the foot is carried forward and upward. In the second phase of the step, the foot descends, reaching forward toward the ground. The foot is then grounded, normally landing on the frog and back third of the foot first. Shoeing or trimming can alter the arc of the foot, changing the character of the horse's stride and affecting his balance and movement.

Each hoof should land in its natural balance, touching the ground evenly without twisting, rocking or striking first on one side and then on the other. If one side of the hoof is longer than the other, that side will strike the ground first, causing a rocking effect. This can result in injuries to the structures of

FIGURE 1 *Arc of the foot:*

a) Normal arc—breakover, flight and grounding

b) Long toe, low heel—long breakover, flat arc

c) Short toe, high heel—short breakover, steep arc

the hoof or to the collateral ligaments of the joints.

For most horses, the closer the horse's feet are to his natural state, the better for his soundness and movement. The hoof angle is especially critical; ideally, the angle of the hoof should be aligned perfectly with the angle of the bones of the pastern. This permits a normal breakover, flight and grounding without creating unnecessary stress on the

FIGURE 2 *Lateral balance:*

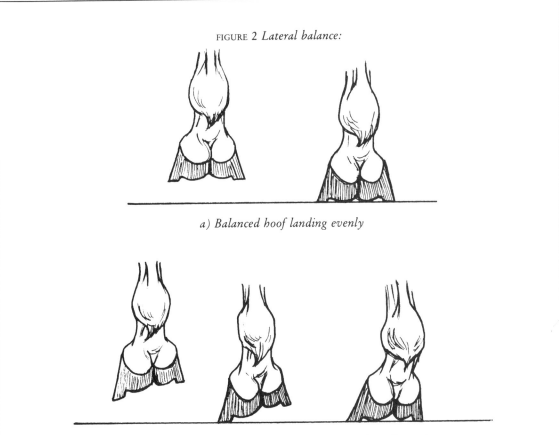

a) Balanced hoof landing evenly

b) Unbalanced hoof lands on high side and rocks to low side.

bones and inner structures of the foot and lower leg.

The angles of the feet also affect the angles of the joints above them, especially in the hind legs. The wrong angle can cause the horse to stand with his hind legs excessively braced, bent or camped out behind him, putting additional stress on all the joints of the hind leg and ultimately affecting his lumbosacral joint, his back and his overall stance and balance. Adjusting the angle of the hoof can give the horse great relief and improve his ability to move and balance himself. This is often a factor in hind leg lameness and back trouble.

Changing the angle of the hoof can alter the breakover and trajectory of the foot in flight. With a long toe and low heel, a "broken-back" angle is created. Breakover of the foot is delayed and the arc of the foot is shorter in the first phase and longer and flatter in the second phase of flight. Some

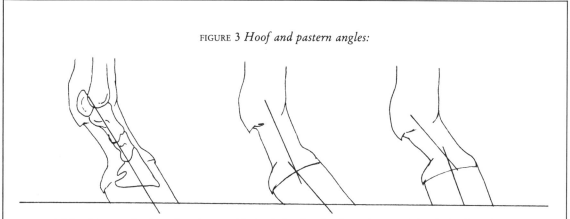

FIGURE 3 *Hoof and pastern angles:*

a) Matching angle of hoof and pastern—bones in alignment

b) Angle broken backward (long toe, low heel)

c) Angle broken forward (short toe, raised heel)

people have their horses trimmed with a low heel and long toe to create the illusion of a longer, flatter stride, but this puts more stress on the deep digital flexor tendon, on the navicular bone and on the edges of the pastern bones as the horse breaks over. This can contribute to tendon injuries, navicular disease and arthritis. A shortened toe and raised heel has a "broken-forward" angle. This causes a quicker breakover and a higher, longer first phase of flight; the second phase is shortened and steeper. This is sometimes done to relieve stress on the tendon, navicular area and pastern bones or to change the balance and angle of the horse's stance.

Long feet (both toe and heel) favor high action and greater flexion in the joints of the leg. Saddle horses that move with high action have their hoofs grown out, and built-up pads add to their length. Both the length of the hoof and the weight of the shoes and pads contribute to the height and flexion of the

stride. In some show classes where natural action is desirable, the rules limit the length of the foot and the weight of the shoes.

Metal shoes add weight, and weight affects the horse's stride and movement. The greater the weight, the more effort is needed to lift the foot and the higher the horse's action. High-stepping saddle and harness horses wear weighted shoes, while horses that should move with long, low action (such as show hunters) often wear lightweight aluminum shoes to minimize the effects of weight. Weight tends to increase the arc of the foot slightly—toe weights are sometimes used on harness racers' shoes to increase the length of stride. Adding weight can increase any tendency to wing in or paddle, especially as the horse tires. Weight also increases concussion as the foot strikes the ground.

Many horses need shoeing for traction, especially if they must maneuver at speed on slippery ground. Calks, studs, toe grabs and

FIGURE 4

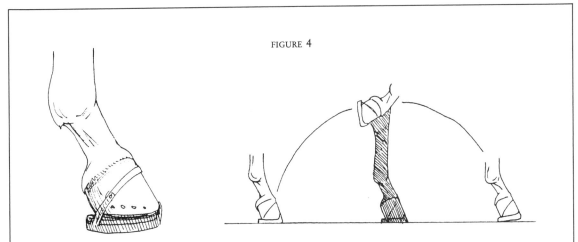

a) Long foot built up with pads and weighted shoe, as for gaited saddle horses

b) High arc with more flexion

borium are all traction devices that can give the horse more stability and allow him to work with confidence that he will not slip. While traction devices give security by biting into the ground, they can also anchor a horse's foot and put strain on his legs if his foot twists against the holding power of the calk. In addition, a horse that interferes, overreaches, kicks or treads on his own foot while wearing calks or studs can injure himself or someone else. Sport horses like jumpers and event horses usually have their shoes tapped so that screw-in studs can be inserted. The rider can put in the best kind of studs for the ground conditions, and the studs are removed immediately after competition. Horses that wear studs or calks should wear bell boots for protection against accidental injuries.

Many horses have crooked legs and tend to wing in or paddle. These horses need skillful trimming and balancing to allow them to ground each foot in its natural balance. Crooked legs can be helped considerably by corrective trimming, but this must be done while the bones are still growing—usually before the horse reaches eighteen months of age. In mature horses, misguided attempts to "straighten" a crooked leg by drastic reshaping of the foot may force the bones out of their natural (although crooked) alignment and cause imbalance, stress and breakdown. Corrective trimming and shoeing must be more concerned with finding the natural balance in which the horse moves best without strain than with trying to make the horse look as if he stands and moves straight. Otherwise the result may be a horse that looks correct but cannot move or stay sound.

To keep a horse sound and moving at his best, the owner needs to practice good foot care. The feet should be picked out and checked daily, and loose nails, rough clinches or loose shoes attended to. Most horses will need their feet trimmed or their shoes reset every six weeks. Letting the feet get too long before trimming or resetting will make the horse move poorly and may cause lost shoes, stumbling or damage to the feet and legs. The owner should discuss the horse's way of going and any changes or problems with the horseshoer; sometimes a consultation with the trainer and/or a veterinarian may be necessary. The owner and the horseshoer should observe the horse standing and moving on a hard level surface to evaluate his stance and way of moving before and after shoeing. Any special shoeing the horse requires should be noted down, along with the best hoof angles and length of foot for that particular horse. Keep in mind that the horse's needs may change from time to time, and both the owner and the horseshoer need to be observant.

12

HOW THE RIDER
AFFECTS MOVEMENT

No horse moves under a rider exactly as he does when free. Carrying the rider's weight and moving in obedience to his signals change the horse's movement. We may also change his movement by our riding techniques, balance, use of aids, bits and equipment and our mistakes or problems.

BALANCE

Perhaps the most important effect the rider has is on the horse's balance. Like the horse, we have a center of gravity—our CG, or balance point. It is located in the center of the body, between the ribs and the pelvis. The CG shifts slightly when we move or change position, but it remains in the same general location. Whether walking, standing, sitting or riding, a person is balanced when his feet and legs are under his center of gravity. If our

CG gets out in front of our feet, we fall forward. If the feet get in front of the CG, we fall backward. When sitting on a chair, a stool or a horse, we can sit balanced or out of balance. If we are out of balance, only the support of the chair (or the horse and saddle) keeps us from falling. When we are well balanced, we are poised to move.

Besides keeping his own balance, a rider needs to be balanced with his horse. When a rider sits so that his center of gravity is directly over that of his horse, he is said to be in balance. A rider who is in balance feels secure and needs a minimum of grip in order to keep his seat. A rider who is out of balance may feel insecure, as if he is always about to fall off. He will have to use grip and strength to stay on and may hold on tightly with his legs, his muscles or his hands. This causes muscle tension in his back, seat and legs. He will often hang onto the reins in order to catch his own balance. The rider's balance

135

FIGURE 1

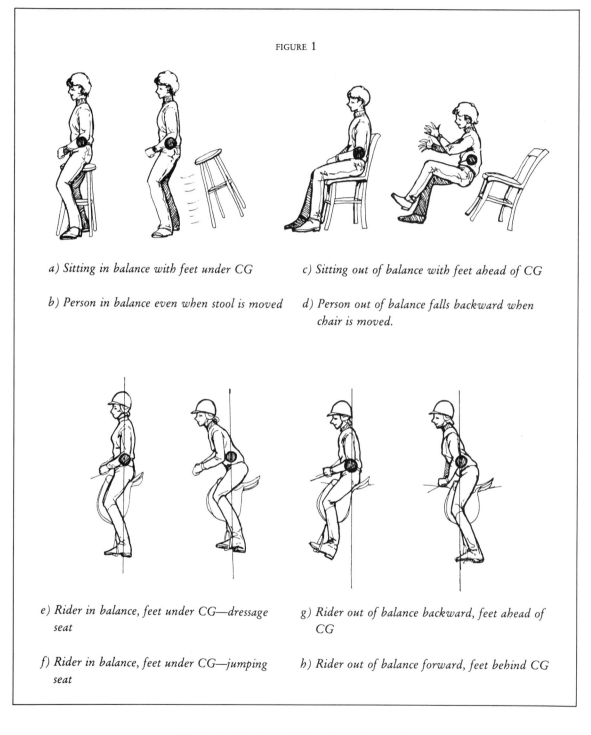

a) Sitting in balance with feet under CG

b) Person in balance even when stool is moved

c) Sitting out of balance with feet ahead of CG

d) Person out of balance falls backward when chair is moved.

e) Rider in balance, feet under CG—dressage seat

f) Rider in balance, feet under CG—jumping seat

g) Rider out of balance backward, feet ahead of CG

h) Rider out of balance forward, feet behind CG

HORSE GAITS, BALANCE AND MOVEMENT

(or lack of it) has a profound effect on the horse's balance and movement.

Horse and rider have a dynamic balance—a balance in motion, not a static balance at a standstill. A rider can ride in motion in three ways: with the motion, behind the motion, or ahead of the motion. When his center of gravity stays over the horse's center of gravity as it moves, he is with the motion and united in balance with his horse. This is the easiest way for both horse and rider to move together. To stay with the motion, the rider must shift his balance and position to go with the horse's changes of balance, which may be small or large, gradual or quick.

If the rider's CG is behind that of the horse, he is behind the motion. This can happen momentarily, as when a rider is "left behind" when a horse unexpectedly jumps forward and the rider fails to move with the motion in time. A rider who is out of balance backwards or "behind his legs" may ride behind the motion. He will sit heavily on the horse's back and will pull on the reins to keep his balance. Unfortunately, this is one of the most common riding faults in all types of riding.

Riding behind the motion on purpose is a technique that may be used to influence the horse's balance, to drive him forward, or as a defensive measure against a buck or a bolt. Even when well executed by a balanced rider, riding behind the motion is harder on the horse's back than riding with the motion. When executed crudely or incorrectly, riding behind the motion can cause the horse to hollow his back, which hampers his engagement, balance and freedom of movement.

When the rider's CG is ahead of the horse's CG, he is ahead of the motion. This may happen when the horse slows down or stops suddenly and the rider falls forward—one of the most common ways of falling off. Riders who make the mistake of leaning too far forward and riding "ahead of the horse" are insecure, and often horses take advantage of them. They encourage the horse to move on the forehand and hamper his balance.

Riding deliberately ahead of the motion is a technique practiced by some riders to relieve the horse's back. It requires good balance and security, and is usually used only briefly.

The rider also needs to keep his CG centered over that of the horse in a lateral sense. Even the slightest sideways shift is felt by the horse and can affect the balance of both horse and rider. A small shift of balance low down in the seat is less risky than leaning far out to the side with the shoulders, and is less likely to unbalance the horse. Swiveling or rotating the shoulders and trunk is a better technique for turning in balance than excessive leaning sideways, as it keeps the rider centered over the horse's CG but is easily felt by the horse.

Like horses, riders have a strong side and a weak side. Tension, tight muscles and lateral imbalance can make a rider crooked. Many riders collapse one hip, drop a shoulder or twist their body to one side without realizing it; often they ride with one stirrup shorter than the other. This causes uneven balance and makes them use the aids more strongly on one side than the other. To ride a horse straight and evenly, the rider must first

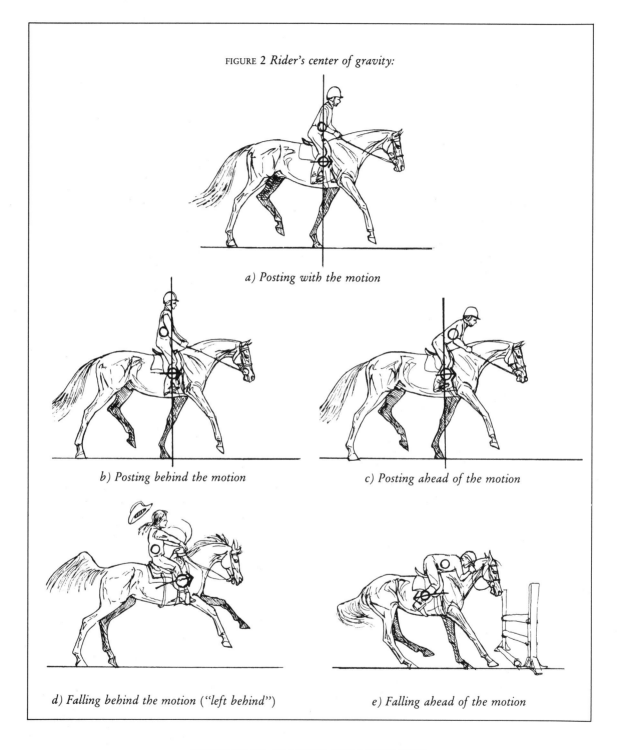

FIGURE 2 *Rider's center of gravity:*

a) Posting with the motion

b) Posting behind the motion

c) Posting ahead of the motion

d) Falling behind the motion ("left behind")

e) Falling ahead of the motion

FIGURE 3

a) Rider in balance in bending turn

b) Rider in balance in turn at speed

c) Rider out of balance in turn at speed

d) Crooked rider seen from behind

straighten himself. Close observation using a mirror or videotape can help to pinpoint the problem. Adjusting the stirrups evenly, lengthening exercises for the shorter side and changing diagonals frequently at the posting trot can be helpful for crooked riders.

How can a rider "balance" his horse? First, we must remember that a 150-pound rider seated on top of a 1,000-pound horse cannot balance the horse—it is the horse that carries his weight and must balance the weight on his back. What the rider can do is influence the horse's balance and encourage the horse to adjust his balance. The best way to do this is for the rider to rebalance himself—bringing his feet and legs directly under his body, balancing his head over his body and lengthening his spine, all in a split second. As the horse feels the rider's quick rebalancing, he will do the same, engaging his hind legs

FIGURE 4 *Horse and rider united in balance; rider's CG remains over horse's CG in all activities.*

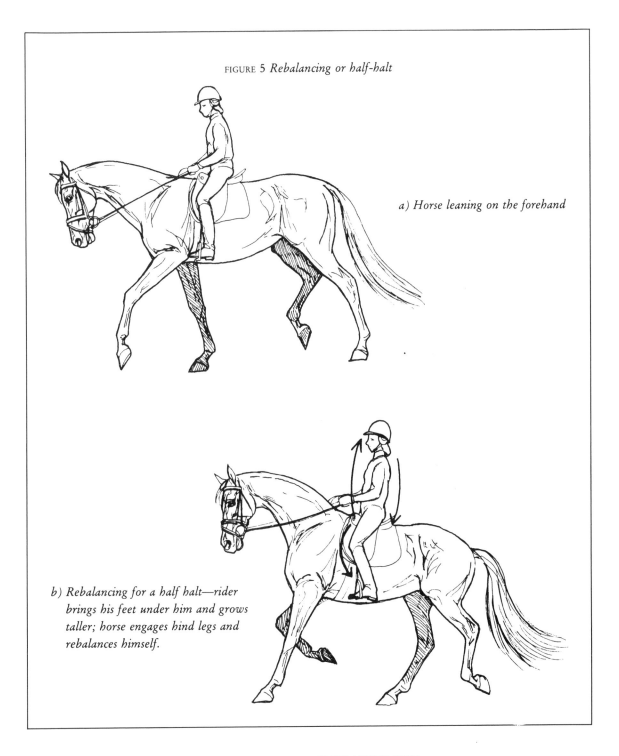

FIGURE 5 *Rebalancing or half-halt*

a) Horse leaning on the forehand

b) Rebalancing for a half halt—rider brings his feet under him and grows taller; horse engages hind legs and rebalances himself.

more, rounding his back and lightening his forehand momentarily. (As you may have guessed, another term for rebalancing is "half-halt".) Neither the rider nor the horse can sustain this rebalancing—it is a split-second effect that must be repeated again and again in rhythm. While the rider's legs, back, seat and hands do play a role in influencing the horse's balance, none of these is as important as the overall rebalancing, which automatically brings them all into play.

SEAT

While the rider's position and seat have already been discussed in terms of balance, there are other important factors in influencing the horse's movement. One of the most important is the freedom and suppleness of the rider's body. A rider who is tight, tense and holding in his muscles, even though he may be in a technically correct position, will be stiff and uncomfortable to his horse and to himself. A free, supple and relaxed rider makes it easier for the horse to move freely and comfortably under him. Tightness and tension are also picked up and reflected in the horse's attitude—horses may become nervous, stiff, resistant or even violent because of the tension they feel in the rider's seat, legs and "feel."

A rider cannot be free and supple if he is out of balance. Sitting even a degree or two ahead of or behind true balance causes tension in the muscles of the legs, trunk and seat as the rider holds himself in place. (This also applies to lateral imbalance, or sitting crookedly.) Finding true balance, whether sitting in the saddle, in a half-seat or posting to the trot, can make a dramatic difference in the rider's freedom, security and ability to follow the horse's movements.

As the horse moves, the alternating swing of his hind legs makes each side of his back rise and drop. His belly swings from side to side, and each side of the back moves forward, back and slightly diagonally. His ribs also expand and contract as he moves and breathes.

If the rider, remaining relaxed but in balance, allows the horse to move his seat bones alternately, it makes it easier and more comfortable for the horse to engage his hind legs and use his back. The rider must let the movement go freely through his body, including his neck and head. If he is "stuck" in any place or if he tries to hold himself still, he will inhibit the horse's movement. Deep breathing, riding to music and riding with the eyes closed (while being led) can help to free the body and allow the horse to move with free, flowing strides. Developing a soft, free "following seat" at the walk is the basis for following the horse's movement in other gaits, especially the sitting trot and the canter. The better the rider learns to allow the horse's movements to go through his body, the more quiet and "still" his seat appears at all gaits. The rider who tries to hold a rigidly "correct" position will stiffen, grip and bounce and interferes with his horse's ability to move well.

Most riders have been taught to "drive with the seat" or "brace the back" as an aid.

While this can be effective, many overdo it, using too much muscle and driving too hard and too long, or falling backward behind their legs. This can make the horse stiffen and hollow his back instead of responding correctly by engaging his hind legs and shifting his balance or moving forward; misuse of the driving seat can give a horse a sore back. The rider should first learn to follow the horse's movements with his seat and body. He can then make small but very quick rebalancings in rhythm with the horse's strides. The use of the seat will become much more brief, light and almost automatic; this is more effective and is much better accepted by sensitive horses. It is much better for producing good movement than driving too severely, too long or out of rhythm.

LEGS AND LEG AIDS

The rider's legs ask the horse for impulsion or energy and engagement of his hind legs; they also help to direct the hindquarters straight or sideways.

Effective use of the rider's leg aids depends first on a correct leg position. When the rider is in a balanced position with his legs underneath him, his calf muscle rests on a sensitive spot on the horse's ribs. A brief twitch of his calf muscle against the horse's barrel stimulates the hind leg on the same side, asking for more impulsion or greater engagement. Squeezing the calf muscle against the external oblique muscles asks the horse to bend laterally; used farther back, it asks for lateral

movement of the hind legs. Touches of the leg or spur on the anterior pectoral muscles ask the horse to engage his abdominal muscles and lift his back in a bascule. If the rider's leg is too far forward or backward or if it wavers around and bumps the horse at random, there can be no precise signal to the horse. This often results in erratic performance or in a horse that is "dead to the legs."

The leg aid must be timed correctly for an effective response. The horse can only respond to a leg aid at the right phase of his stride. For more thrust, he must respond while the leg is on the ground and pushing off. For greater engagement, he can only respond while the leg is pushing off and swinging through the air; when it is grounded and supporting weight, it cannot engage more. If we want the horse to move the leg sideways, he can only do this while the leg is pushing off and moving through the air—not while it is stuck on the ground. Timing is essential.

When the horse moves, he places one hind leg (let's say the right hind leg) on the ground. His belly swings out over that leg (to the right), and that side of his back rises. Meanwhile, the other hind leg is swinging forward through the air (engaging). If the rider learns to feel the swing of the belly, he can time his left leg aid to catch the left hind leg as it pushes off and swings through the air. This is easiest to feel at a big-striding walk—just relax and notice the swing of the belly out to the right, again and again with the rhythm of the stride. If you let your left leg "follow the belly," it can give a brief leg aid as the belly swings out to the right—

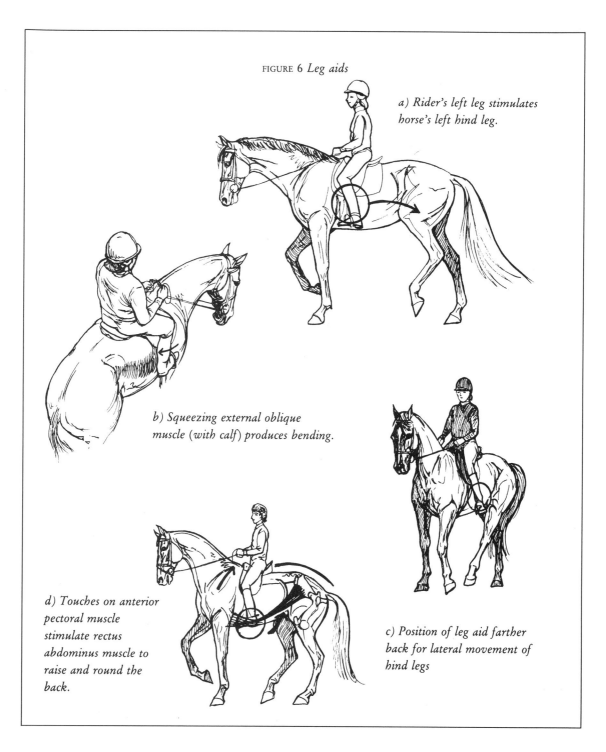

FIGURE 6 *Leg aids*

a) Rider's left leg stimulates horse's left hind leg.

b) Squeezing external oblique muscle (with calf) produces bending.

c) Position of leg aid farther back for lateral movement of hind legs

d) Touches on anterior pectoral muscle stimulate rectus abdominus muscle to raise and round the back.

HORSE GAITS, BALANCE AND MOVEMENT

imagine that you want to push the belly an inch or so farther out. When you time the left leg aid correctly, you will feel the horse lengthen his stride and engage his hind leg more deeply instead of just quickening his walk with short strides. It is possible to time the leg aids by looking at the shoulder, but learning to time them by feel is more useful and more effective.

In the walk, alternating leg aids (following the belly) can be used to ask for increased engagement. In the trot, the aids can be timed best at the posting trot. If you post on the correct (outside) diagonal, you will be rising when the outside foreleg and inside hind leg push off and swing through the air. This is the time to use the inside leg aid. (If you prefer to use the inside leg aid when you sit, you must change to the inside diagonal.) In the sitting trot, the rider can "post mentally" until he feels the timing. In the canter, the swing of the belly is almost as easy to follow as in the walk; the inside (leading side) leg aid is used at the moment when the belly swings outward. For lateral work, the rider must first feel when the hind leg he wants to influence is coming off the ground. He can then use a lateral leg aid (slightly farther back) to send the hind leg sideways as it engages.

Leg aids must be light, brief and accurate to be effective. Some horses have learned to ignore the rider's leg aids. If you prolong your leg aid in an effort to make it stronger so the horse will respond, you will stiffen up and the horse will probably bounce your leg off his stiff side, ignoring you even more effectively. Instead, sensitize the horse to the

FIGURE 7 *Timing leg aids:*

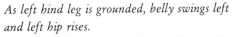

As left hind leg is grounded, belly swings left and left hip rises.
Right hind leg is swinging forward (engaging).
Rider's right knee drops and right leg goes back and inward.

leg aid by tapping his side with a crop or whip as close as possible to the spot where you apply the leg aid. For this to work, you must give a brief, light leg aid and then tap him within one second of the leg aid. Then, use the light leg aid again. The object is to make the horse more sensitive to your leg aids, not to teach him to scoot forward because he sees you have a whip. Lazy horses may react better if you wear spurs, but remember, spurs are to be used to touch, not to poke holes in your horse!

HANDS AND REINS

Bits, reins and the hands that hold them are important in controlling, guiding and influencing the horse. In addition, the horse's head and neck are his "balancer"; the position, carriage and gestures of the head and neck have a profound effect on the way the horse moves and on his balance. The bit and the way the rider uses it have much to do with the way the horse uses his head and neck and, consequently, his overall movement.

The horse must have some freedom to use his neck and place his head in the best position for his balance and movement. Head position has a lot to do with the horse's vision—in some positions, he may be effectively blind to what is in front of him. He may need to use his head and neck to make a gesture to save his balance. If the rider's hands restrict the horse's use of his head and neck too much, it inhibits his movements. Accidental abuse of the bit often occurs when a rider loses his balance and saves himself by pulling on the reins. This can make the horse protest by throwing his head, overbending or otherwise defending himself, or he may resign himself to the constant pull, lean against the bit and become heavy in hand and

hard-mouthed. Either will make him clumsy, stiff and awkward to ride.

The horse must be comfortable in his mouth and with his rider's rein aids to move well. The pain of a severe or ill-fitting bit will make a horse stiff and tense, even if he is not actively resisting. (You may behave the same way when you have a toothache!) Jerking, sawing, pulling or other severe use of the bit will cause the horse to recoil in fear and distress—besides being abusive, these are ruinous to good movement.

Most bits are designed to act correctly when there is a straight line from the bit to the rider's elbow. If the rider's hands rise above this line, the bit acts upward; if his hands drop below the straight line, it acts downward. Either way changes the action of the bit, often making it more severe. When it acts in a straight line, it is "neutral" and acts as it is designed to do. (The straight line from elbow to bit depends on the height of the horse's head. If the horse carries his head high, the rider will have to raise his hands to keep a straight line; if the head is low, his hands will be lower.)

Maintaining the straight line from elbow to bit encourages the horse to use his head and neck naturally and avoids distorting the carriage of the neck by forcing the head into a set position with a severe use of the bit.

There are several methods of using the bit to control the horse and influence his movement. During a horse's training, he may move from one stage to another as he becomes better able to understand and respond to the rider's aids. It is important to choose

FIGURE 8 *Bit and rein angles:*

a) Straight line from bit to elbow—bit acts neutrally

b) Line broken upward—bit acts upward in corners of lips

c) Line broken downward—bit acts downward against bars of mouth

the best method for the activity as well as for the horse's stage of training. All of these methods depend as much on the rider's use of his balance, seat and legs as they do the bit and rein aids, and affect the horse's balance and movement, not just the way he responds with his mouth or his head.

SIMPLE LOOSE-REIN CONTROL

In the most elementary stage, the horse is ridden with loose reins and is given simple signals to stop or turn by brief tugs backward or sideways. Nonleverage snaffles or hackamores or a mild combination bit like a pelham or kimberwicke are most appropriate. These suffice for slow and simple riding with a calm horse moving in his own natural balance. The advantage of this method is that the horse is free to use his head and neck naturally and find his own balance with little interference from the rider. The disadvantage is that the rider cannot do much about the horse's way of going, and it is inadequate for activities demanding fast stops and turns or changes of balance. Most horses ridden this way move on the forehand. It is used for the earliest stages of training young horses, for beginning riders and for simple trail riding and pleasure riding.

FIGURE 9

a) Simple loose-rein riding

b) Passive (soft) contact. Horse stretches rein with extended head and neck; rider follows head and neck gestures.

RIDING ON CONTACT

The next stage is soft or passive contact. The rider adjusts his reins and uses his legs to encourage the horse to move forward with longer strides. This causes the horse to extend his head and neck and make contact with the bit and the rider's hands. The bit is usually a mild snaffle. The rider maintains the soft contact by elastically following all the movements of the horse's head and neck. He can ask for halts or turns by momentarily squeezing his hands and stopping the following motion instead of pulling. The horse responds by making gradual transitions and by flexing or relaxing in the mouth, but not with real collection. The advantage of this stage is that the horse is encouraged to move with more engagement and an extended neck in a natural balance, and the rider has more control without pulling or forcibly changing the horse's head carriage, balance or use of his body. It can be a useful stage in teaching the horse to accept the bit and trust the rider's hands. However, it is easy for the horse to move too much on the forehand. Passive contact is used in training green horses and sometimes for riding hunters.

ON THE BIT

The next stage requires flexion and rebalancing as the horse's response to the bit. The rider's legs and seat ask the horse to reach forward, engaging his hind legs and lengthening his back and neck. He meets the soft but firm resistance of the rider's fixed hands. ("Fixed" is a relative term—the hands are always elastic to some degree, but they do not give and follow the movement of the horse's head as in passive contact.) As the horse pushes against the resisting hand, he learns to yield, or give to the bit, by collecting himself—by relaxing his jaw, flexing at the poll and especially by flexing his lumbosacral joint and hip joints and rounding his back in collection. This creates more engagement, a change of balance and more collection, with the horse using his back as a lever to raise the forehand and making a neck-telescoping gesture. The horse actively seeks a contact with the bit and will reach out and down to find the bit if the rider lengthens his reins. He is said to be "on the bit." This can be done to a small degree (seen in green horses just learning the technique), to a larger degree (hunters, lower level dressage horses and pleasure horses) or to a much greater degree (show jumpers, high level dressage horses and horses working in true collection). This work is begun in a mild snaffle; a double bridle may be introduced at a later stage.

This stage is the most useful for improving the horse's movement and balance and his ability to move well under a rider at all gaits. It demands more of the rider as well as the horse—as the horse's balance and responses become fine-tuned, the rider's own balance, timing and sensitive use of the aids become critical. The rider must ride in balance and have an independent seat; he must be free, balanced and responsive in his own body or he will block the horse's movement. This may require great strength, not to "muscle" the horse into obedience, but to maintain a perfect position while following the huge movements of a talented horse and waiting for the moment when the horse truly "comes through."

Self-Carriage

The ultimate goal of this stage is self-carriage, a state in which the horse finds a balance in which he can remain collected and carry his rider with only the lightest of contact or even on loose reins. Self-carriage cannot be attained without calmness, rhythm, impulsion, straightness, suppleness and all the other desirable gait qualities.

Self-carriage is developed as the horse advances in his training and becomes stronger and more supple in his back and hindquarters. As he learns to move with increased engagement and balance, he needs less support from the rider's hands. He also becomes confirmed in his rhythm and tempo and maintains his own best working rhythm without needing prompting from his rider. In dressage horses, self-carriage is sought at a fairly advanced level, as the horse becomes strong and supple enough to maintain a collected balance through various movements. In other specialties, the horse finds an optimum working balance which is usually not as collected as that of an advanced dressage horse, but in which he can move his best with the least effort from both horse and rider.

A classical test of self-carriage is "giving and re-taking the reins." The rider momentarily stretches his hands forward to the horse's crest, giving up the contact, and then smoothly returns his hands to their normal position. If the horse is in self-carriage, his balance and carriage will be undisturbed. If he rushes or falls out of balance, the rider knows that his horse was not truly in self-carriage, and he (the rider) may have been hanging on the reins or allowing the horse to lean on the bit. During this test, the rider must keep his own position, balance and rhythm intact, and must support the horse's movement with his forward-driving aids.

LOOSE REIN AND NECK REINING

Western horses, polo ponies and other horses that work on loose reins may go through a different but parallel process. They are usually started with a nonleverage bit or hackamore—a snaffle bit, bosal or side-pull hackamore. After the initial elementary loose-rein stage, they often skip the stage of soft but positive contact and go directly to flexion and collection on a light rein. For western horses, this may mean a mild curb or pelham; some continue in a snaffle or a hackamore. The rider uses brief, light touches on the bit in a check-and-release method instead of steady contact. The horse is taught to engage his hindquarters and collect himself all in one movement in stops and downward transitions in response to the rider's shift of balance and a quick check and release on the

FIGURE 10

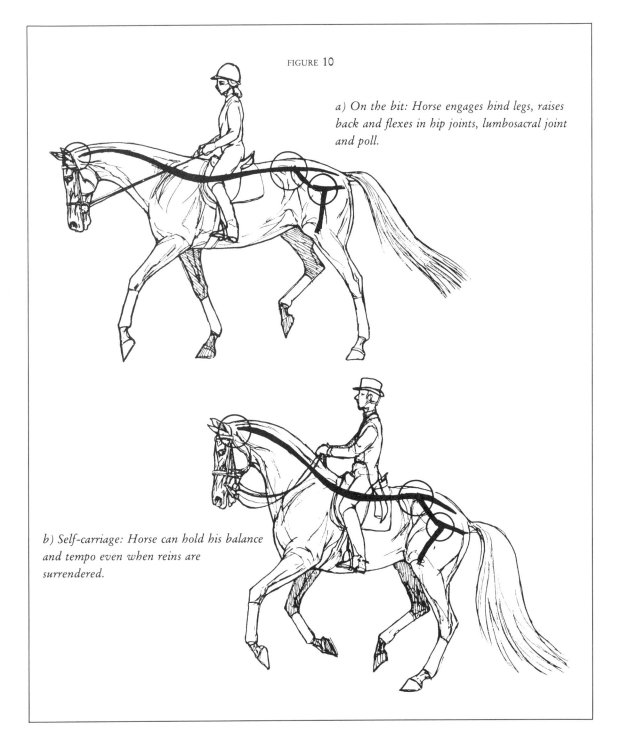

a) On the bit: Horse engages hind legs, raises back and flexes in hip joints, lumbosacral joint and poll.

b) Self-carriage: Horse can hold his balance and tempo even when reins are surrendered.

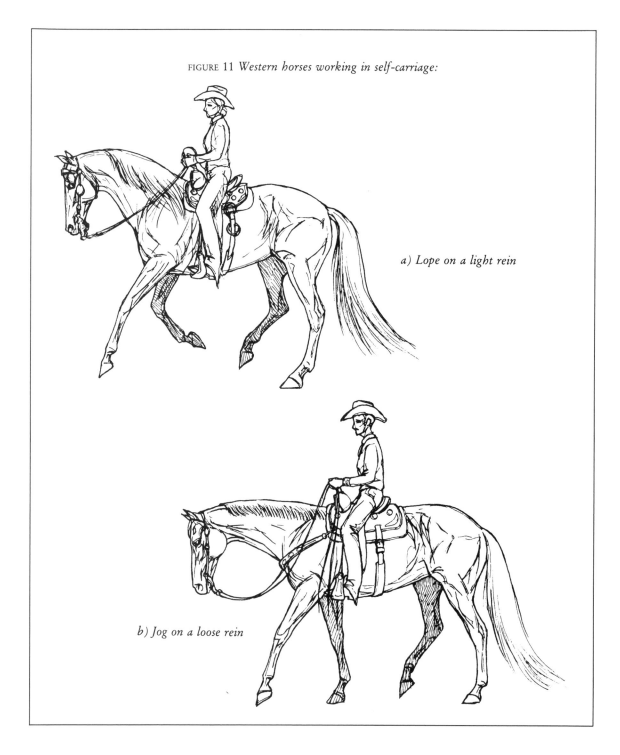

FIGURE 11 *Western horses working in self-carriage:*

a) Lope on a light rein

b) Jog on a loose rein

HORSE GAITS, BALANCE AND MOVEMENT

bit or hackamore. He is trained to neck-rein—that is, to turn on his hindquarters in response to a quick, light touch of the rein against one side of his neck. He is expected to move in self-carriage on loose reins from a very early stage; this is possible because he is not asked for as much impulsion, as short a frame or as big movement as an advanced dressage horse. The western horse trained this way is ridden with a loose rein or a light rein (a rein with a slight dip or slack in it, but with a very light contact). He responds as much to the balance of the rider as he does to the quick, brief and very light touches on the bit. Strong contact, long, hard pulls backward or against the neck or hanging on the reins will quickly ruin a loose-rein trained horse, especially if he is abused with a curb or other leverage bit.

HEAD-SETTING

Head-setting is a different approach to the use of the bit. Some trainers believe in "setting the horse's head" at an early stage of training, sometimes even before the first ride. The horse is bitted up with a snaffle bit, surcingle and side reins, sometimes with check reins. He learns to relieve the pressure of the side reins by tucking his nose in and assuming an arched and flexed position of the neck. The horse may be longed or driven in long lines while he is learning the desired head posture; later he may be ridden with a martingale, draw reins or another head-setting device. Some riders lower their hands and

seesaw on the reins, which has the same effect. This teaches the horse to carry his head in a certain posture and to respond to bit pressure by tucking his nose into a "headset" position whenever he feels bit pressure. It is a common practice among trainers of gaited saddle horses, some English pleasure horses and western show horses, and is sometimes used by trainers in other disciplines when attempting to deal with a problem horse. It is most often used for horses that have a great deal of natural impulsion and desire to go forward; setting the head is intended to provide control and to channel the horse's energy into collection, while maintaining a disciplined and orthodox head carriage.

The problem with head-setting is that it inhibits correct movement and can damage the horse. Head-setting does not teach the horse to engage his hind legs, to flex his lumbosacral joint or his hip joints, or to round and raise his back. The horse may learn to comply with the head-setting device (or the lowered, seesawing hands of his rider) by flexing his neck and tucking his nose in, but his hind legs may be disengaged, his back may be dropped and he may be crooked, stiff and unbalanced. Moving with a hollow back can cause damage to his back, hocks and hind legs, and forcible head-setting can cause stiffness and pain in the poll, neck and shoulders. As the horse withdraws from the mechanical pressure of the side reins, he may learn to overflex, retract his neck or lean and bore against the bit instead of collecting himself correctly. A set head inhibits the horse's use

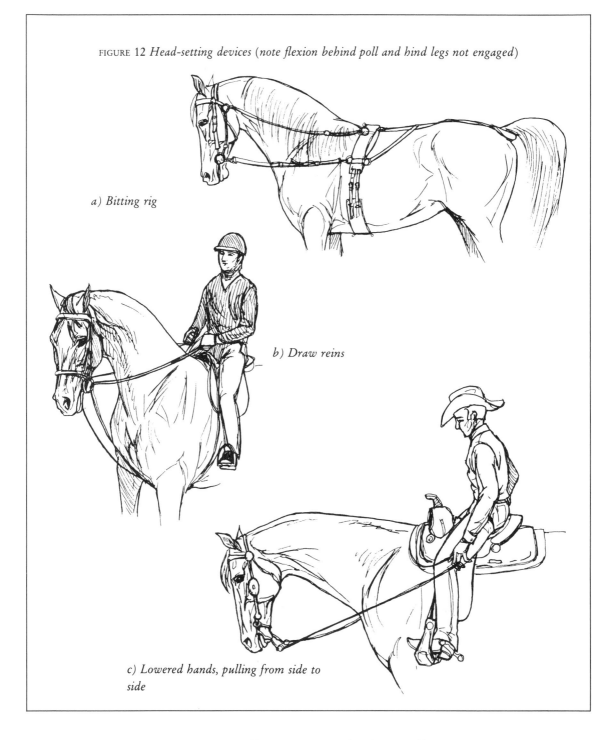

FIGURE 12 *Head-setting devices (note flexion behind poll and hind legs not engaged)*

a) Bitting rig

b) Draw reins

c) Lowered hands, pulling from side to side

of his back, which prevents him from engaging his hind legs and hindquarters effectively. It also teaches the horse to retract his mouth and neck backwards, away from the bit; this can make it very difficult to establish contact or a more natural head carriage. It can cause stiffness and tension that block free, elastic movement and interfere with rhythm. Too often, it results in a horse that is superficially arched and rounded in front and strung out or worse behind. At worst, it may force the horse into a unnatural way of moving that can destroy his movement and ultimately cripple him.

Head-setting is a symptomatic approach to collection; the trainer is starting at the wrong end. Head carriage should be the *result* of engagement and collection, not the starting point. By paying more attention to develop-ing engagement and good use of the back, along with appropriate flexion in response to the bit, the horse's mechanism is strengthened and he learns to use himself fluently. Martingales, draw reins and, yes, even head-setting devices may occasionally be useful in correcting a horse that has learned incorrect responses to the bit. However, to use these to correct a problem and enhance the horse's movement instead of spoiling it requires much knowledge, experience and judgment and above-average riding skills. Those trainers who are capable of using draw reins and head control devices to improve a horse without causing damage usually have little use for them; too often, it is the novice and the heavy-handed butcher who have no business using them who are eager for quick-fix devices!

13

IMPROVING YOUR HORSE'S MOVEMENT—SOME PRACTICAL TIPS

The way a horse moves is determined to some extent by his genetic heritage, his conformation and soundness and his type of movement. You can't make a short, low mover into a high-actioned park horse, and a poor or mediocre mover will never move as well as the horse that is gifted with superior conformation and movement. However, good riding and training can improve any horse's way of going, and there are some practical things you can do to help your horse reach his potential. These exercises can help your horse to become stronger, fitter and more responsive as well as moving better in whatever type of riding you do.

RHYTHM FIRST!

Dressage trainers have a saying, "Rhythm first!" What they mean is that a horse cannot move freely, easily or even relax until he set-

tles into a good working rhythm in his gait. If his rhythm is inconsistent, quickening and slowing the tempo, he is very hard to ride.

Tense, excitable horses often speed up the tempo until they are "running" in any gait. Other horses slow to a crawl, hopping momentarily into a faster pace when the rider gets after them and subsiding to the minimum effort as soon as they can. Some break down to a slower gait at any opportunity. Either problem is penalized in the show ring and makes the horse difficult to ride.

When a horse finds his own best working rhythm, he is able to move in balance, to swing his legs more freely and to relax his back and neck. He breathes evenly and can continue longer without tiring. Moving at a quicker or slower rhythm, or, especially, an unsteady rhythm, is frustrating, inefficient and uncomfortable.

The rider can help by developing his own

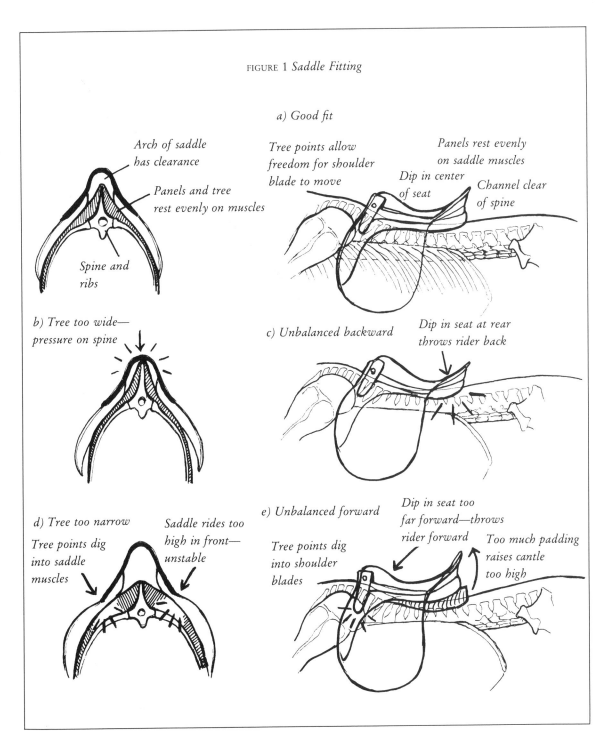

FIGURE 1 *Saddle Fitting*

a) *Good fit*

Arch of saddle
has clearance

Panels and tree
rest evenly on muscles

Spine and
ribs

Tree points allow
freedom for shoulder
blade to move

Dip in center
of seat

Panels rest evenly
on saddle muscles

Channel clear
of spine

b) *Tree too wide—*
pressure on spine

c) *Unbalanced backward*

Dip in seat at rear
throws rider back

d) *Tree too narrow*
Tree points dig
into saddle
muscles

Saddle rides too
high in front—
unstable

e) *Unbalanced forward*

Dip in seat too
far forward—throws
rider forward

Too much padding
raises cantle
too high

Tree points dig
into shoulder
blades

IMPROVING YOUR HORSE'S MOVEMENT

sense of rhythm and by finding the horse's best working rhythm and helping him stay in it. This is best done at the posting trot, but it also applies to the other gaits.

To improve your own and your horse's rhythm, try humming, whistling or even singing to the beats of the gait as you ride. You can also ride to music from a tape player or the radio. Use your aids in repeated short "pulses" to the beat of the music and the rhythm of your horse's gait. Time your posting to the beat of the tune, and your horse will learn to follow it. For a quick, tense horse, slow your own rhythm and post slower than he wants to trot. This works better than pulling on his mouth to slow and steady him. For lazy horses, apply brief leg aids in rhythm to keep them from letting their rhythm drag down to a crawl. Learn your horse's best rhythm for each gait so that you can help him find it and stay in it.

CHECK YOUR SADDLE

Many horses are sore in their backs or hampered in their movement because of a poorly fitted saddle. An unbalanced saddle throws the rider off balance, which makes it impossible for the horse to carry him well.

A saddle must fit the horse without pinching, rocking, creating pressure points or pressing on the horse's spine. This means that the tree must be the right width and shape for the horse's back. A too-wide saddle sits down too low and causes pressure sores on the withers. A too-narrow saddle rides high in front, throwing the rider backward and digging the tree points into the horse's back and shoulder muscles. The saddle must be balanced so that it does not throw the rider backward or forward, and the lowest part of the seat should be in the center. It must be placed correctly so that it rests on the saddle muscles, allowing room for the spine and for the movement of the shoulder blades.

Check saddle fit by putting the saddle on the horse without a saddle pad. No part of the saddle should touch the spine; you should be able to fit two fingers between the saddle and the withers when the rider is mounted. Run your hand over the back of the horse's shoulder blade, under the front of the saddle. It should not pinch or dig into the back and shoulder muscles. Look at the balance of the saddle from the side. If it tilts backward or forward, it is out of balance and may hurt the horse's back as well as throw the rider out of balance.

Some horses are more comfortable and move better with a back protector pad. These pads, made of neoprene or other materials, cushion the effect of the saddle and the rider's weight and let the horse's back muscles move more comfortably. Be careful not to unbalance a saddle by stuffing too much padding under it.

The saddle must fit the rider, too. Too small a saddle, too large a saddle or the wrong length of stirrup can put the rider out of balance, making him uncomfortable and hindering the horse's movement.

RIDE IN BALANCE

Perhaps the single most important thing a rider can do to improve his horse's movement is to ride in balance. Most riders ride somewhat out of balance—usually behind the motion. This makes them come down more heavily on the horse's back than they realize and forces them to unconsciously tighten their back and grip with their legs. Riding too far forward puts the rider ahead of the motion and encourages the horse to move on the forehand. It can also cause low back pain in the rider.

To the horse, it means that his back is under strain, his rider feels tight and stiff and inhibits his movements, and he may get thumped in the back or grabbed in the mouth. He may become tense and fretful, he may get a sore back or he may just take care of himself by moving short, stiffly and as little as possible. He will not want to engage his hind legs well or raise his back in a bascule if the rider is out of balance.

A good balancing exercise is the "teeter-totter." Sit on your seat bones in the lowest point of the saddle. With your feet out of the irons, "teeter" slightly backward and forward, just a few degrees. Do your tilting from the seat bones, not up in the waist, and keep your back long and straight. Let the teetering get smaller until you find the balance point, with your body at true vertical. This helps balance and align the parts of your upper body, from your seat bones up. It will also help you sit correctly on your seat bones.

FIGURE 2 *Riding in balance*

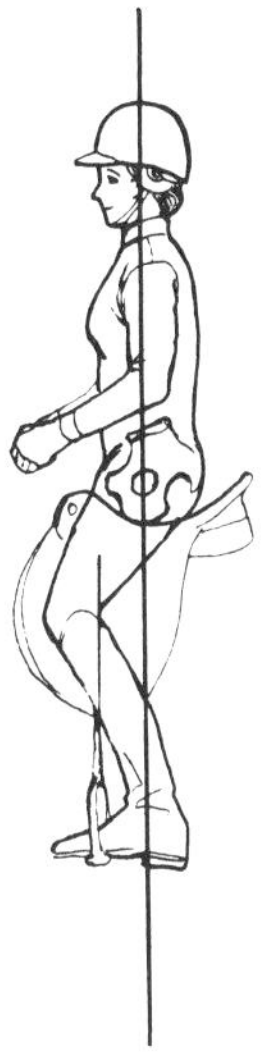

a) Sitting in balance
Vertical line through head, hip and foot; pelvis vertical

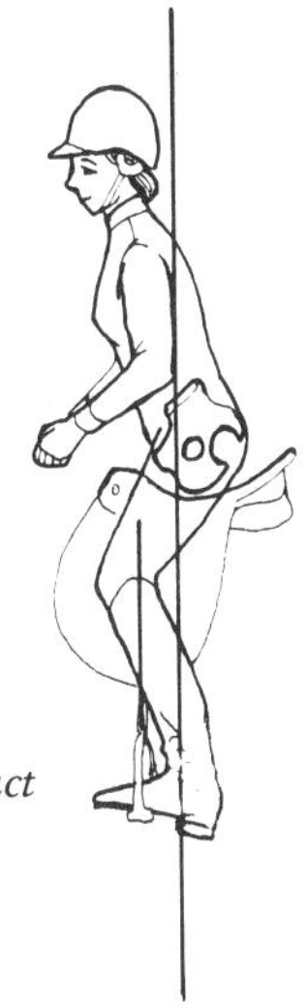

b) Half-seat or two-point contact in balance

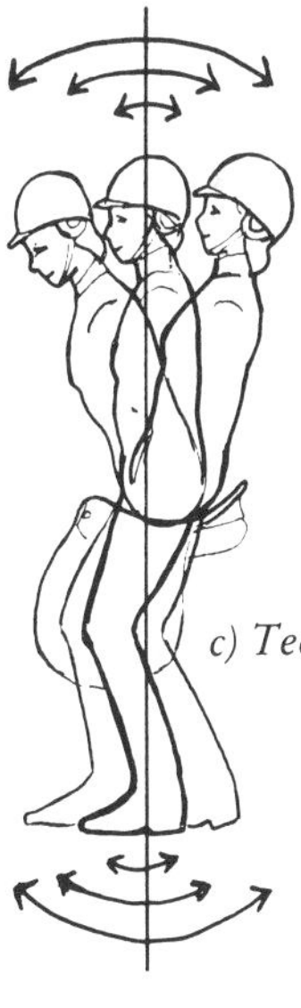

c) Teeter-totter exercise

The classical balance exercise with feet in the stirrups is half-seat (also called two-point contact). You must have the correct stirrup length or you will find it impossible to keep your balance. If you can stay up in the half-seat without holding on, tensing up or gripping with your legs, you have found perfect balance. While working on this exercise, it is all right to grab the horse's mane or to hold onto a neck strap, but *never* catch the reins to save your balance!

In motion, use the half-seat to check your balance. If it is hard to get up or if you sit down unexpectedly, you were behind the motion. If you topple forward, you are ahead of the motion. Bringing your feet accurately under your body makes it easier to find true balance. This exercise helps you sharpen your sense of balance.

You can practice riding in half-seat at the walk, trot and canter. (Western, dressage and saddle seat riders will need to take a more vertical position in half-seat than jumping riders.) At the posting trot, try alternating posting and half-seat every few beats. As the exercise gets easier, you have come into better balance. Practicing riding in half-seat without reins (on a longe line or a steady horse) is an excellent exercise to develop good balance and an independent seat. Working up and down gentle slopes and riding over cavaletti in half-seat will further develop your balance.

LET YOUR HORSE MOVE YOU

Many riders are tense, tight and stiff—sometimes from nervousness or from trying to hold themselves in a perfectly correct position, or from simply trying too hard. A stiff, tight and unyielding seat prevents the horse from using his back freely, and can make him stiff, tense and resistant. It also makes it impossible to sit comfortably to the trot and canter.

To free your seat, first check your balance. (You cannot be free to go with the movement if you tighten up because you are out of balance.) Next, breathe deeply. This frees and relaxes your body. Ride at a walk, with your feet out of the stirrups. If you can get someone to lead your horse for a few minutes, you can ride with your eyes closed. As your horse walks, notice the way the horse moves your seat bones. Let him move each seat bone forward and backward, up and down, around in a circle. You may feel the movement in many other parts of your body, too. As you allow the horse to move you, he will lengthen and free his strides, relax his back and swing his hind legs farther under his body.

Freeing your seat is easiest in the walk, but the same principle applies in all gaits. If you or your horse become tense when you are working in a sitting trot, go back to the following seat at the walk for a few minutes to free up your seat and his back again.

FIGURE 3

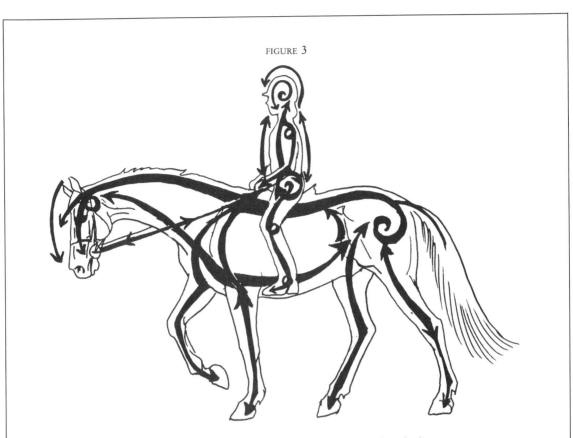

Movement of horse produces movement in rider's body

STRAIGHTEN UP!

Horses and people are never completely symmetrical. We all have one side that is stronger and usually tighter and stiffer than the other. Horses move crookedly and most riders sit unevenly and apply their aids more strongly on one side. Some horses are one-sided—they cannot bend in one direction or may be unable to canter on one lead. Becoming more aware of straightness can help you sit straighter, use your aids more evenly and develop and free both sides of your horse.

To straighten your horse, you will first have to straighten yourself. If a mirror is available, halt your horse squarely and look at yourself from the front. If not, you may have to rely on videotape, photos or an instructor's eye. Which shoulder is lower? Does one hip look higher? Does one stirrup appear longer?

Your stronger (and tighter) side will be

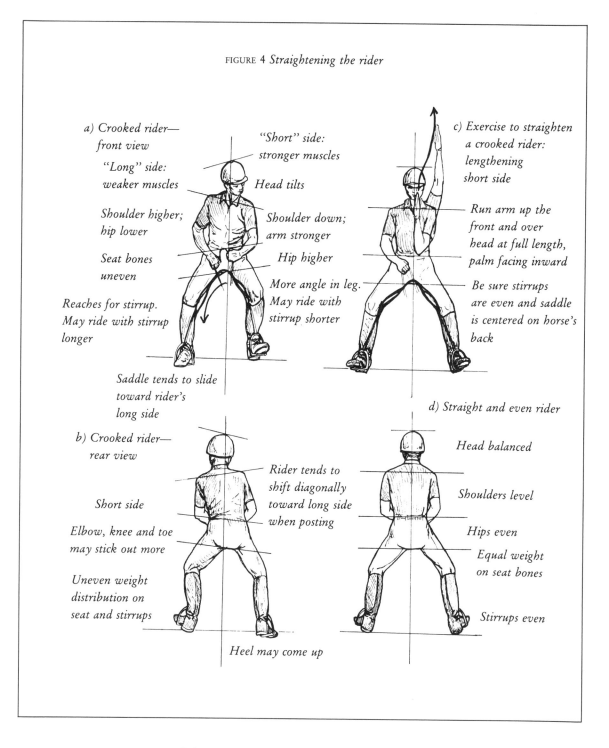

FIGURE 4 *Straightening the rider*

*a) Crooked rider—
front view*

"Long" side:
weaker muscles

Shoulder higher;
hip lower

Seat bones
uneven

Reaches for stirrup.
May ride with stirrup
longer

"Short" side:
stronger muscles

Head tilts

Shoulder down;
arm stronger

Hip higher

More angle in leg.
May ride with
stirrup shorter

Saddle tends to slide
toward rider's
long side

*c) Exercise to straighten
a crooked rider:
lengthening
short side*

Run arm up the
front and over
head at full length,
palm facing inward

Be sure stirrups
are even and saddle
is centered on horse's
back

*b) Crooked rider—
rear view*

Short side

Elbow, knee and toe
may stick out more

Uneven weight
distribution on
seat and stirrups

Rider tends to
shift diagonally
toward long side
when posting

Heel may come up

d) Straight and even rider

Head balanced

Shoulders level

Hips even

Equal weight
on seat bones

Stirrups even

HORSE GAITS, BALANCE AND MOVEMENT

162

shorter. That shoulder will drop and you may ride with that stirrup shorter. The saddle will slip toward your longer (weaker) side, and you may post diagonally toward your weaker side.

To straighten your body, make sure your saddle is square over the horse's spine and that your seat bones are even in the center. Make sure the stirrups are even. On your strong side, raise your arm up over your head, palm facing inward. This lengthens the muscles on the short side and places your weight evenly over your seat bones and stirrups. You can ride at a walk and at other gaits with your arm over your head, until you can feel yourself become straighter. As you become more even, your horse may feel more free on his stiffer side, too.

Other exercises that help even up a one-sided horse and rider are: changing diagonals every two or three strides at the posting trot; frequent changes of direction with gentle "S" turns; the "forward and out" exercise described later in this chapter, and shoulder-in (when correctly executed). Above all, the rider must become aware of his own straightness and must avoid leaning when turning or trying to move the horse sideways.

HALF-HALT

A half-halt, or rebalancing, is a brief call for the horse to pay more attention to the rider and to rebalance himself. A half-halt asks the horse to engage his hind legs more deeply for that stride and to lighten his forehand. It also improves the rider's balance and puts him in closer touch with his horse for that moment. Half-halts are used to prepare a horse for a movement, to ask him to listen to the rider, to improve his balance and engagement, and to correct certain undesirable behaviors, like leaning on the bit.

To execute a half-halt, the rider momentarily rebalances himself, bringing his legs more directly underneath his body and allowing his spine to lengthen. (This is described on page 139.) A half-halt may emphasize the use of the rider's leg aids, a brief push with his seat, or a short action of one or both reins. For certain purposes, a rider may want to emphasize the action of the seat, back, legs or reins, but any use of the rein is always supported by the forward-driving aids of the legs or the seat, and the rider must be careful not to "clash his aids"—pulling backward while driving the horse forward.

Half-halts must be executed in brief pulsations, followed by an immediate relaxation of the active aids. Nobody can sustain a half-halt—trying to push, drive or hold for more than a split second makes the rider stiffen up and can cause the horse to resist instead of responding correctly. Half-halts should be executed in rhythm with the gait; if they are quick, short and light, they can be done at every stride or every other stride.

A good way to learn to use half-halts is to rebalance just before and immediately after each corner. Notice the horse's balance through the corner as you feel him respond to your rebalancing—it may feel like he "picks himself up" for a moment. Next, try a series of half-halts timed in rhythm with his strides, or with every other stride if you are just learning how to use half-halts. If you emphasize the forward drive by using a little extra leg pressure with each half-halt, you may feel your horse pick up more energy and prepare to make an upward transition to a faster gait. If you emphasize the balance of your seat (try pulling your navel backward toward your spine for a split second as you think of growing taller), you may feel your horse lift his back and adjust his balance under you. Emphasizing the relaxation of your seat after each half-halt may cause your horse to "melt" into a smooth downward transition or a halt. Remember that a good half-halt is done mostly by the rider's body; the hands are only the "icing on the cake." As you become better at half-halts and your horse gets more responsive to them, you may find that he responds to your rebalancing without needing rein pressure. When you can make "no hands" half-halts, transitions and even halts, you will have fine-tuned your own balance and your horse's response to it.

Use half-halts whenever you feel your horse begin to lean or become heavy on his forehand, or if he is going too fast. They are also an effective way to call for your horse's attention or prepare him for a new movement. A good half-halt is so small a movement that an onlooker (or a judge!) will not see you do anything. (This is how good dressage riders get their horses to perform with "invisible aids.") You can also use half-halts, or rebalancing, to teach your horse to collect himself and to balance better before a turn or when riding downhill.

SENSITIZE YOUR HORSE TO LIGHT LEG AIDS

Horses should respond to light, brief leg aids; these are easier, more effective and more comfortable for both horse and rider. Some horses learn to "tune out" the rider's leg aids, ignoring all but the strongest driving leg. If the rider gives longer and stronger leg aids to make the horse listen, the problem only gets worse. A better answer is to sensitize the horse to a lighter, more accurate leg aid. If your horse can feel a fly light on his ribs, he can feel a very light leg aid—he needs to be taught to respond to it correctly and immediately.

To sensitize your horse, first test his response. Squeeze, nudge or kick as hard as you must to put him into a trot from a walk. Now, on a scale of 0 to 10, how much leg did it take to get him to respond? If he trotted without being touched, that is a 0; 10 is the absolute maximum leg aid you can give. If it takes a 6 to get him to trot, your goal will be to get him to respond to a lower number—a lighter aid.

At a walk, give him a brief, lighter leg aid—a 4. If he does not trot immediately, do not increase your leg aid or make it longer. Instead, repeat the light aid and immediately reach back and hit him once with a crop beside your leg. To be effective, you must hit him within one second of your leg aid, and you must hit him just hard enough to surprise him into a trot. Be very careful not to jerk his mouth as he jumps into a trot, and pat him and praise him *immediately* when he trots. Let him trot for a way, then drop back to a walk and try the lighter leg aid again. Be ready to pat and praise him instantly and generously if he trots from the lighter aid, and be ready to correct him instantly with the crop if he ignores the leg aid or dawdles. He hasn't learned his lesson until he will trot off promptly from your light leg aid alone (a 4), without needing the crop. Never wave the crop or threaten him with it—you want him to respond to your light leg aid, not to seeing a crop in your hand. When he responds to a 4, try a 2 and repeat the process.

With an occasional reminder, your horse can learn to respond promptly to reasonably light leg aids—1 to 4—instead of waiting until you use a 10 or a 19!

FORWARD AND OUT

If your horse cuts corners, drifts toward the center or leans in on his turns, he needs to learn how to move forward and out from an inside leg aid. This controls corner cutting and lays the foundation for bending and lateral work; it also can help you to teach your horse to engage his inside hind leg, raise his back and stretch into the bit.

To teach your horse to move forward and out, halt parallel to the track but about ten feet inside the rail. You will ask him to move off with your inside leg aid, applied in brief

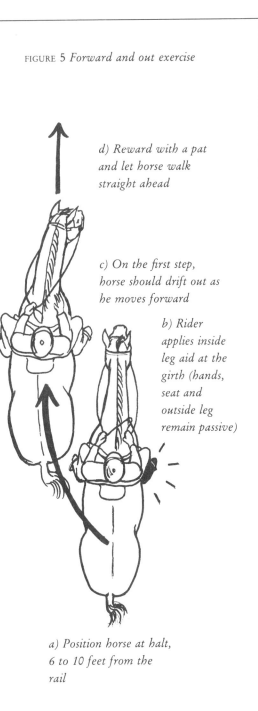

FIGURE 5 *Forward and out exercise*

d) *Reward with a pat and let horse walk straight ahead*

c) *On the first step, horse should drift out as he moves forward*

b) *Rider applies inside leg aid at the girth (hands, seat and outside leg remain passive)*

a) *Position horse at halt, 6 to 10 feet from the rail*

pulses in its normal position just behind the girth. (Do not move your leg back, or it may confuse him.) Leave the reins loose; at first, you want to isolate your aids and teach him to respond to the inside leg aid only, not your reins or seat.

When he responds to the inside leg aid, he should begin to walk and simultaneously drift out slightly toward the rail. If he does this, pat him and praise him and allow him to walk on freely. Don't keep after him with the inside leg aid—it is the *initial* response that is important. He does not need to continue to move sideways after that first step. Don't use the reins any more than you have to—you want him to learn to respond to your inside leg aid, not your reins. By the same token, don't lean or drive him sideways with your seat, either. Reward him instantly and generously when he gets it right.

At first, most horses will make mistakes. Instead of moving forward and out, they may walk straight ahead, go sideways instead of forward or perhaps push inward against your leg aid. If this happens, stop the horse gently but promptly and repeat the inside leg aid. You may have to help him a little bit with the reins to show him that he should move outward, or tap with a crop beside the inside leg aid. Use many small leg aids instead of a long, hard aid. Be careful not to pull backward on his mouth—forward is just as important as out. Repeat the exercise until he is moving forward and out promptly in both directions.

Once the horse moves forward and out from the halt, he can learn to do it in motion. As he walks, follow the swing of his belly at each stride. Apply a brief leg aid as the belly swings *out* (left leg as the belly swings out to the right). He should move forward with a bigger stride as he moves out. Remember, it is the immediate response on the first stride that counts—not continuing to move sideways. You can then do the exercise in the trot, being careful to time your inside leg aid when the inside hind leg is off the ground. (If you are posting on the outside diagonal, use the inside leg as you rise.) When the horse moves easily forward and out on long reins, he can be asked to move forward and out into the contact of the rider's hands.

This exercise helps the rider to time his aids effectively and teaches the horse to respond with his inside hind leg. As he responds to the inside leg aid, he learns to engage his inside hind leg farther under his body. This helps him stretch his back and neck and reach out into the bit; it also sends him into the contact of the rider's outside aids. The slight outward movement helps him to take some of the weight off his inside shoulder. The outward shift of his ribs teaches him to bend slightly around the rider's inside leg and look in the direction of the turn. This exercise lays the foundation for correct bending from the hind legs, without overbending the neck or putting the horse behind the bit by concentrating too much on the front end.

USING SHOULDER-IN TO DEVELOP YOUR HORSE'S MOVEMENT

Shoulder-in is a classical dressage exercise that has long been used to supple, strengthen and improve the movement of dressage horses. It can also help horses that are not dressage specialists. When properly applied, it is one of the most effective exercises for developing suppleness, straightness, better collection and increased engagement of the inside hind leg. Often the quality of the gaits and the use of the horse's body show noticeable improvement after working in shoulder-in. Shoulder-in can also be used to correct crookedness, to counter resistances and to ride a horse past a scary object without shying. The eighteenth-century French master de la Guérinière, who invented the movement, called it "the first and last lesson a horse must be taught."

In the shoulder-in, the horse moves forward with his hind feet traveling straight along the track. He is bent around the rider's inside leg and his shoulders and forelegs are brought about one step to the inside of the track, so that his outside shoulder is in front of his inside hindquarter. He looks away from the direction in which he moves.

In a good shoulder-in, the horse must step farther under himself with his inside hind leg. This increases the engagement and teaches the horse to carry more weight on the inside hind leg, which helps in developing collection. The horse's spine must be in alignment (without leaning, overbending the neck or "falling out" over the outside shoulder), and the back, withers and base of the neck are raised, developing a good bascule. He flexes laterally at the poll and appears evenly bent around his rider's inside leg. The horse responds to the rider's inside leg aid and is regulated by the outside rein; he is "on the aids"—light, supple and responsive. He maintains the pattern, rhythm and tempo of his gait and remains in balance.

To begin shoulder-in, ride through the end of the arena with your horse moving forward on the bit and bending around your inside leg. At the corner, ride a small circle (approximately 10 meters, or 33 feet, in diameter) to prepare your horse. As you complete the circle, use your inside leg at the girth to ask your horse to move sideways for one step. (Your outside leg remains slightly behind the girth to prevent the hindquarters from swinging out.) Move both hands slightly to the inside and turn your shoulders to the inside—this brings the horse's forelegs and shoulders one step to the inside. At each stride, your inside leg asks the horse's inside hind leg to engage more and sends him slightly sideways; your outside rein, along with the turn of your shoulders, keeps his shoulders in position. A brief half-halt at each stride (emphasizing the inside leg and the outside rein) keeps the horse from leaving the track. The inside rein can help to gently lead the shoulders to the inside, but it must not overbend the horse's neck or overpower the effect of the outside rein.

In the beginning, you should only ask for a few steps of shoulder-in at a time. Always

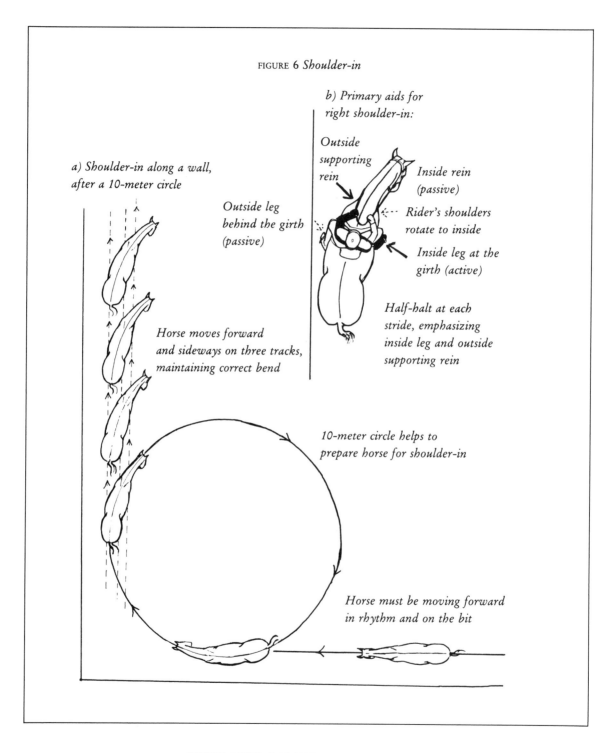

FIGURE 6 *Shoulder-in*

*b) Primary aids for
right shoulder-in:*

*Outside
supporting
rein*

*Inside rein
(passive)*

*Rider's shoulders
rotate to inside*

*Inside leg at the
girth (active)*

*a) Shoulder-in along a wall,
after a 10-meter circle*

*Outside leg
behind the girth
(passive)*

*Half-halt at each
stride, emphasizing
inside leg and outside
supporting rein*

*Horse moves forward
and sideways on three tracks,
maintaining correct bend*

*10-meter circle helps to
prepare horse for shoulder-in*

*Horse must be moving forward
in rhythm and on the bit*

HORSE GAITS, BALANCE AND MOVEMENT

FIGURE 8 *Correct and incorrect shoulder-in*

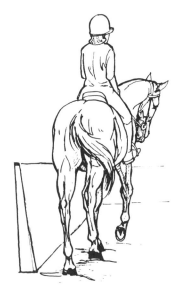

*a) Shoulder-in correctly ridden—
horse moves on three tracks, evenly
bent, with back raised
and correctly aligned*

*b) Incorrect and damaging lateral work—
"cranking" horse forcibly sideways
with inside rein, spur and twisted body results
in stiff, hollow and uncoordinated
movement with torque in hind legs*

*c) Incorrect—rider leans and "cranks"
inside rein; horse falls out
through outside shoulder and bends
incorrectly (neck only)*

send the horse forward in an energetic gait after a lateral movement. While classical shoulder-in is ridden in collection on three tracks (the outside foreleg is placed in front of the inside hind leg) or sometimes at an even greater angle, a less experienced horse may be ridden at a slightly smaller angle and with less collection. Practicing a few steps at a time frequently works better than trying to keep the horse in the movement for a few too many strides, and a milder form of the exercise performed fluently will do more for the horse than a more extreme version that is a struggle.

The most common rider error in shoulder-in work is to "crank" the horse with the inside rein in an effort to make the horse step sideways with his forelegs. This produces a false bend in the neck only and teaches the horse to "pop his shoulder" and fall out through his outside shoulder. The horse is sent forward and sideways by the rider's inside leg, never by the rein. A related fault is leaning, tilting or contorting the body by trying to push the horse sideways with the seat. This puts the rider out of balance and makes it impossible for the horse to align his spine correctly and to engage his inside hind leg well. Instead, he will stiffen and resist. Remember that the rider's inside leg, not his seat or reins, is the primary aid—the horse must move from his inside leg into his outside rein. If the horse doesn't respond sufficiently to the inside leg aid, it should be reinforced with a tap of the whip or a touch of the spur, but the rider should never resort to leaning, cranking the inside rein or contorting the body.

Shoulder-in is usually described as a movement along the long side of an arena, but it can be very useful when ridden on a circle. The aids are essentially the same; it may help to think of riding a circle with the forelegs making a slightly smaller circle than the hind legs. Spiraling in and out on a circle is a related exercise that can be used to prepare the horse and rider for shoulder-in. Try riding a few steps of shoulder-in on a circle or turn before a canter depart or before asking for lengthening the strides in the trot; it often results in better impulsion and engagement. A mild shoulder-in can be used to straighten the canter, especially for horses that carry their hindquarters to the inside. It is also useful to ride past an object that the horse would like to shy away from, as it turns the horse's head away from the object and keeps him under the control of the rider's inside leg and outside rein.

Good shoulder-in work can help a horse use his body better and improve his movement, but bad shoulder-in can spoil his movement and even cause physical damage. When a horse tries to perform shoulder-in in a stiff, forced and uncoordinated way, he stiffens his back instead of rounding it in a nice bascule. Forced lateral movement puts twisting forces on the joints of the hind legs, especially the hock and stifle joints. This can cause great pain and injury to the back and hind legs, and can even result in serious damage to the joints. A twisted, uncomfortable horse will develop all kinds of resistances to defend himself from the demands of his rider, and becomes more difficult to ride instead of

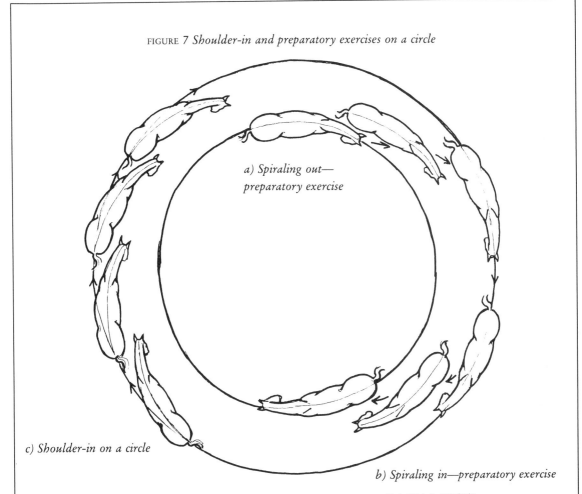

FIGURE 7 *Shoulder-in and preparatory exercises on a circle*

*a) Spiraling out—
preparatory exercise*

c) Shoulder-in on a circle

b) Spiraling in—preparatory exercise

more supple and a better mover. Hence the cardinal rule for lateral work is: "Do it right or don't do it at all!" If you are unsure about how to ride a shoulder-in or how to teach it to your horse, you need personal help from a qualified instructor or trainer. Even riders with much experience in lateral work need an educated eye from the ground to keep their work correct and to keep little faults from developing into serious problems.

CAVALETTI

Work over cavaletti, or ground poles, has long been a basic part of jumping training. It can also help the movement of horses that are never expected to jump.

Cavaletti are a series of poles set on the ground at intervals, called a grid. When correctly spaced, they regulate the horse's stride. He must flex the joints of his legs more in order to step over the poles and must use extra thrust, or impulsion, to clear the raised cavaletti at a trot. Most importantly, cavaletti work encourages the horse to engage his hind legs and round and stretch his back in a bascule. This strengthens his hindquarters, abdominal and back muscles and develops freedom of movement in the hind legs. It also teaches the horse to pay attention to where he steps and look where he is going. Working over cavaletti at a walk without a rider is sometimes useful as physical therapy for certain back and hind leg problems (consult your veterinarian first). Cavaletti can be practiced at the walk, trot and canter, but walk and trot work is most useful for improving movement.

The spacing of the poles is very important. The horse should be able to step in the middle of the space between the poles without reaching, tripping or skipping a pole. For average-size horses, start with poles spaced at 3' to 3'6" for walking and 4' to 4'6" for trotting. A ground helper must watch the horse's stride through the cavaletti, then adjust the distance until it is comfortable for him. For safety, the poles should be fixed so that they will not roll under a horse's foot, and the horse should wear protective boots or bandages.

Cavaletti work can begin with leading and later longeing the horse over three to five poles at a walk. When he has learned to work calmly, staying in rhythm and stretching his back, he can begin trotting. A calm, steady rhythm and a relaxed attitude are essential—if he rushes through the poles with his head up and his back stiff, he is not improving his movement and he can get hurt. Under saddle, the rider should stay up off the horse's back in a half-seat, or two-point position, as the horse goes over the cavaletti. He must allow the horse to round his back and stretch his neck out and down in a bascule.

Cavaletti work is strenuous and hard on unfit joints and muscles, so don't overdo it. Three to five poles are enough, and four to eight passes through the grid are usually plenty. Start with the poles resting on the ground and raise them very gradually—only after the horse has worked over the lower poles for six days or more. Cavaletti should not be raised to more than six to eight inches for this type of work—even this height requires more thrust and greater bending of the joints of the legs. Walking over raised cavaletti (three or four passes) is a good addition to a warmup once the horse has learned how to relax and stretch his back as he steps over the poles.

TRAIL RIDE

Trail riding, or hacking out, is one of the most enjoyable ways to improve your horse's movement. Riding outside refreshes both horse and rider and keeps them from becoming bored and ring sour. It is the closest form of riding to the horse's natural life, and horses that do lots of trail riding are often sounder, more resourceful and more sensible than horses confined to ring work. Many show horses can benefit from work outside,

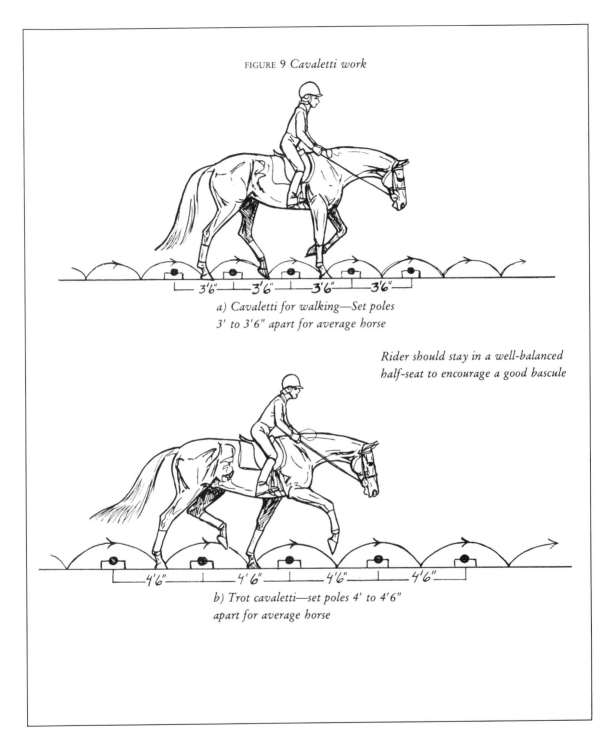

FIGURE 9 *Cavaletti work*

*a) Cavaletti for walking—Set poles
3' to 3'6" apart for average horse*

*Rider should stay in a well-balanced
half-seat to encourage a good bascule*

*b) Trot cavaletti—set poles 4' to 4'6"
apart for average horse*

both for their movement and for their attitude.

When riding out, encourage your horse to walk out. A good ground-covering walk is a pleasure to ride, and it will develop your horse's hindquarters and ability to engage his hind legs. Feel for the swing of his belly as he walks, and use alternating leg aids to ask him for longer strides in a steady four-beat rhythm. Encourage him to stretch his neck and back by allowing him long reins, but don't ride with dangerously sloppy reins.

Hills and rolling terrain are great developers of movement. Walking up hills develops the horse's hindquarter muscles; trotting up hills develops muscle, wind and impulsion. Always stay up off his back in a half-seat when going uphill—sitting down can cause a sore back. When going downhill, slow your horse down and insist that he frequently re-balance himself so that he rounds his back and engages his hind legs. Going downhill crooked or hollow-backed and high-headed can injure your horse; good balance is not only good practice, it is safer for both of you.

You can use natural obstacles to practice bending and handiness. Try weaving in and out of a row of trees, or follow a winding trail. Use your inside leg to keep the horse from knocking your knee on a tree; you will also be practicing "forward and out," or bending. Stepping over fallen logs or tree roots is much like cavaletti; your horse should stretch his neck down, raise his back and flex his hind legs. Stay up off his back to help him.

Many horses are more motivated to move forward outside the ring; this is a good way to develop lengthened strides at the trot. Keep him in balance and in his best working rhythm—don't let the horse fall into a "running" tempo and sprawl forward, even if it feels like a powerful trot. You will not like this habit when you ask for a true extended trot!

Cantering and occasional hand-galloping outside are wonderful for developing a free, forward and balanced canter. Be very aware of balance and rhythm, especially when you allow the strides to lengthen to a gallop. A good galloper seems to drop lower to the ground and his stride becomes longer, not faster. Letting the horse scuttle as fast as he can makes him hot and crazy but does nothing for developing his stride and balance. The horse's attitude should be your guide—if he becomes agitated, do more calm, quiet work at the walk and trot and omit the fast work.

INDEX

Numbers in *italics* indicate illustrations.